IN THE HEART OF THE
BITTERROOT MOUNTAINS

THE STORY OF
THE CARLIN HUNTING PARTY
SEPTEMBER-DECEMBER, 1893

by
Abraham Lincoln Artman Himmelwright

17, 678

Mountain Meadow Press
1993

IN THE HEART OF THE BITTERROOT MOUNTAINS
THE STORY OF THE CARLIN HUNTING PARTY
SEPTEMBER-DECEMBER, 1893

by Abraham Lincoln Artman Himmelwright

Based on the G. P. Putnam's Sons 1895 edition of
In the Heart of the Bitter-Root Mountains

Significant portions of the Introduction and the Post-script were reprinted with permission from "Tragic Trek" by Edmund Christopherson, *Montana, The Magazine of Western History*, Autumn, 1956, pp. 46-55.

Cover art by Mary Lou Pethtel

Published by Mountain Meadow Press
Printed in the United States of America

Library of Congress Catalog Card Number 93-078127
ISBN 0-945519-16-8

Carlin Party Found

Destitute and Crazed with Suffering

Special Dispatch
Missoula, Montana,
November 25, 1893.

Greatly to the surprise of everyone the Carlin party of young New Yorkers who have been besieged in the Bitterroot Mountains, southwest of Missoula, for nearly two months, has been found more dead than alive.

The account of their sufferings, as related by a courier just arrived, is harrowing in the extreme.

They were famished, without horses or provisions, barefooted, only the soles of their shoes remaining, and were scant of clothing.

Hemmed in by impenetrable snow banks and after several ineffectual attempts to escape, the party became resigned to its fate, trusting to Providence for relief.

Lt. Elliott found the men in a sad condition verging on insanity. He administered what immediate relief was at his command. Colgate, he learned, was still behind, having fallen in his ability to keep up with the party. Carlin believes that the man will not ever be found alive.

When the men were found they were totally bewildered and were wandering about aimlessly on a snow-covered plateau on which the depth of snow averaged fourteen feet. Their horses had long since stampeded and their provisions were exhausted, save what little they carried in their pockets. The little band of brave men were making their last and final effort to get out when found, and thirty-six hours later would have found them dead.

TABLE OF CONTENTS

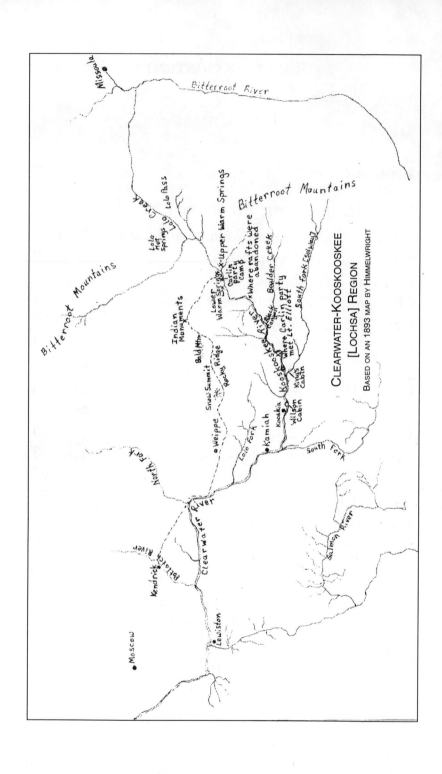

CLEARWATER-KOOSKOOSKEE
[LOCHSA] REGION

BASED ON AN 1893 MAP BY HIMMELWRIGHT

Introduction

At mile 148 along North Central Idaho's Highway 12 wilderness corridor, a white wooden cross marks the century-old burial site of George Colgate, a stark postscript to the story of the tragic circumstances that surrounded his death. In the autumn of 1956, *Montana* magazine journalist Edmund Christopherson reviewed, with both fascination and horror, records of the Carlin hunting party with whom Colgate had come to the Bitterroots. Christopherson's words, which follow here, will introduce you to the time period and events upon which this intriguing story is based.

Tragic Trek

1893 was a lively year, the year of the [national economic] panic. The Northern Pacific Railway was in the hands of receivers, who had announced wage cuts all around. Chicago was having its World's Fair. Oklahoma's Cherokee Strip was being thrown open. Congress was hassling over the perennial silver problem. Newspapers printed hints on how to pull stumps and features on the declining use of snuff in favor of the new-fangled, paper-wrapped smokes they called cigarettes. The ads touted Skookum Hair Root Grower and cuts of horses vainly trying to split a pair of Levi's copper-riveted spring-bottom pants. Beer dropped to 5¢ a large stein on Missoula, Montana's Front street skid row, while elsewhere this Garden City's citizens fomented a State University and talked of becoming a "Boston of the West."

William E. Carlin, for whom the Carlin Hunting Party was called, was the 27-year-old, mustachioed son of Brigadier General W. P. Carlin,

Commander of U. S. Troops at Vancouver at the time. Young Carlin had grown up on army posts in the Northwest and, as a relative of top brass, had frequently gone along on Army exploring and mapping expeditions into backcountry.

His friend, A. L. A. (Abraham Lincoln Artman) Himmelwright, then 28, was a civil engineering graduate of Rensellaer, with experience in surveying for the Northern Pacific R. R. before he returned to engineering jobs in New York.

The third easterner in the party was John Harvey Pierce, 30, Carlin's brother-in-law, who helped his father, a White Plains, New York, doctor with his investments.

As a guide they hired Martin P. Spencer, a 27-year-old Iowa refugee from asthma, with eight years of dude catering to his credit.

Because he'd been with him on previous safaris, Carlin insisted on taking as cook and general handyman 52-year-old George Colgate, a slight Englishman who at the time was acting Justice of the Peace at Post Falls, Idaho.

They were well equipped. Besides their mounts there were five packhorses loaded with supplies and three dogs. On September 18 they took their gear out of a boxcar at Kendrick, Idaho, and shoved off for the Lolo Trail. This was country that Capt. John Mullan, some thirty years earlier, described as being the most difficult, rugged, severe, and broken mountainous country he'd encountered between the plains of the Missouri and the plains of the Columbia. Prophetically, an old timer they encountered at Brown's Creek said, 'Reckon you'll have a hard time in the snow so late in the fall.' The party's chief reaction was resentment at being taken for tenderfeet. The next day, as they left the wagon road for the trail, they found six inches of snow on the ground. It was tough, tedious, steep, crooked going, with hundreds of fallen trees blocking the way. The horses cut their feet on the logs and rocks and left a bloody trail in the snow.

Early into the trip—after several days' attempts to hunt, signs of a mysterious ailment in George Colgate, and steady rains suggesting accumulating snows on the return trail—Spencer warned that the party might get snowed in for the winter. At one point he urged the party to begin their return to Kendrick immediately. But the easterners wanted more hunting.

Indeed, as predicted by Spencer, when the party finally did decide to leave the Bitterroots, their horses were blocked by three-to-four feet of snow on the trail. What followed has become one of the most controversial and frequently retold tales of trial and tragedy in the heart of the Bitterroot Mountains.

Chapter I

Clearwater Country and the Lolo Trail

High on the western slope of the Bitterroot Mountains of eastern Idaho, hundreds of miniature streams dash their foaming waters fresh from fields of perpetual snow into four main forks which form the headwaters of the Clearwater River. Skirting the bases of lofty mountains, surging against the naked faces of projecting cliffs, leaping over precipices, and ever and anon struggling with innumerable boulders planted firmly in their beds—the roaring forks of the Clearwater River follow their sinuous course westward. Scores of creeks and branches, draining a territory thousands of square miles in area, add constantly to their volume. These tributaries have for ages been eroding the solid granite. Deep gulches and canyons have been formed, many miles in extent, converting the whole region into a wild, tangled mass of irregular mountain ranges and spurs, whose ragged crests and peaks tower to altitudes of four to eight thousand feet above the sea. The less precipitous slopes are covered with a dense growth of pine, fir, cedar and tamarack, while many steep hillsides with northern exposures have impenetrable thickets of pine and fir saplings. Occasionally, large rockbound areas are found, covered with moosebrush, and here and there, sometimes clinging to almost vertical hillsides and often occupying the tiny flats nestling by the sides of the tortuous watercourses, are dense patches of brush yielding in their season a profusion of berries.

This veritable wilderness, whose forests abound in game and whose streams teem with trout, covers an area equal to that of the State of West Virginia. It can boast of not having a single permanent habitation of man, not even a wagon road. The Lolo Trail, now almost abandoned and so poorly defined that only expert woodsmen and guides can follow it, is the best route by which this region may be entered or traversed. On account of the exceptionally rough character of the country, the trail, instead of following the watercourses, as is usually the case, follows the undulating and convoluted crests of ridges, often requiring ascents and descents of several thousand feet. Into these wilds the whistle of the locomotive has never penetrated; their pristine solitudes are undisturbed by the ring of the settler's axe. Even the wandering Indian hesitates before risking a journey into the mountain fastnesses, and bold indeed is the occasional prospector or hunter who ventures into their unexplored depths.

The Indians were, of course, the original explorers of this wild region, and there are, in the more accessible localities, unmistakable evidences of their early presence. Whether they had permanent villages or remained for any considerable periods of time in those localities is, of course, unknown; but the rigorous climate, and the excessive snowfall to which the district is subject during the winter months, probably drove them out of the mountains at that season.

The first white men who visited the Clearwater country were Lewis and Clark, who traversed it in their famous exploring expedition to the Pacific Ocean in 1805-6. It is most interesting to observe that their notes and descriptions of the country as found in their original narrative are as fresh and true to nature as when they were first penned.

After the exit of Lewis and Clark, the Rocky Mountain region of Montana and Idaho was not revisited by white men for forty-seven years. At the expiration of that period—in 1853—the explorations and surveys "to ascertain the most practicable and economical route for a railroad from the Mississippi River to the Pacific Ocean" were begun, under the direction of the War Department. Four principal parties were organized and sent into the field, each being assigned a certain territory in which to operate. Isaac I. Stevens, Governor of Washington (the General Stevens who was killed at Chantilly in 1862), was placed in charge of one of these parties, and it was in the prosecution of this work that A. W. Tinkham, in 1853, and Lieut. John

Mullan, in 1854, traversed the Clearwater country from east to west, following approximately the old southern and northern Nez Perce trails respectively. Lieutenant Mullan subsequently (1858-1862) was engaged in the exploration, location, and construction of a military wagon road from Fort Benton on the Missouri River to Fort Walla Walla on the Columbia River. The necessary examination of the intervening territory—which embraces the Clearwater basin—in order to solve the problem of location intelligently, involved an enormous amount of the most difficult and laborious exploration. Referring to the character of this locality, Captain Mullan recently said: "I have traveled over much of the Rocky Mountain region from the 39th to the 49th degree of latitude north, and from the plains of the Missouri to the plains of the Columbia, but nowhere did I ever meet with so difficult, rugged, severe, and broken or mountainous country as that situated between the Tinkham route of 1853, and the Coeur d'Alene route (by me) in 1854."

For many years the vast region comprising the St. Joseph, the Clearwater, and the Salmon River basins and the main range of the Bitterroot Mountains formed an impassable barrier between the settlements east and west of it. The necessity of opening a more direct line of communication between Virginia City, Montana, and Lewiston, Idaho, than the Mullan road afforded caused the Government in 1866 to make an appropriation of fifty thousand dollars for that purpose. The same year a reconnaissance was made and the route located by Wellington Bird, assisted by George B. Nicholson and Oliver Marcy. It was soon ascertained that the character of the country was such that the appropriation in hand was barely sufficient to open a good trail suitable for the passage of packtrains. The evident desirability of even so unpretentious a thoroughfare led to its immediate construction, and the following year the trail was completed. The route selected was, briefly, as follows: From Lewiston over already existing wagon roads on the south side of the Clearwater River to Schultz's (now Greer's) Ferry; from that point a trail was graded eastward, following approximately the old northern

Nez Perce trail, which parallels the Kooskooskee [Clearwater and Lochsa Rivers] to the main range of the Bitterroot Mountains at a distance of from ten to twenty-five miles. The trail then crosses the headwaters of the Kooskooskee, passes thence over the Bitterroot range at Lolo Pass, and descends the eastern slope of the mountains along the Lou-Lou [Lolo] fork of the Bitterroot River in Montana to Fort Missoula. Near that point the trail intersected Mullan's military wagon road, along which, as well as on other previously constructed roads, the route led to Virginia City. That portion of the route between Schultz's Ferry and Fort Missoula became known as the Lolo Trail, taking its name from a creek of that name which empties into the Clearwater River from the north. As civilization has advanced, those portions of the Lolo Trail from Missoula to the Lou-Lou [Lolo] Warm Springs on the east, and from Greer's Ferry to the Musselshell Creek on the west, have been superseded by wagon roads. The total length of the trail from Weippe, the last settlement at the present time on the west, to Missoula is about one hundred and thirty miles.

After the Northern Pacific Railroad was built along the Clark's fork of the Columbia River, a better means of communication between points east and west of the Clearwater country was secured by that route, and the Lolo Trail, though more direct, fell into disuse.

After the battle at White Bird Canyon during the Nez Perce war in 1877, Chief Joseph and his remnant of hostile Indians retreated northward, crossed the Clearwater River, and passed over the Lolo Trail to the Bitterroot River in Montana. The pursuit of the Indians through this region involved difficulties which the uninitiated cannot comprehend. A brief extract from General Howard's interesting work, *Chief Joseph*, will serve to assist the reader to form an idea of the country and the condition of the trail only ten years after it had been built:

> It does not appear far to the next peak. It is not so in a straight course, but such a course is impossible. 'Keep to the hog-back!' That means there is usually a crooked connecting ridge

between two neighboring mountain heights and you must keep on it. The necessity of doing so often made the distance three times greater than by straight lines; but the ground was too stony, too steep, the canyon too deep, to attempt the shorter course. Conceive this climbing ridge after ridge, in the wildest kind of wilderness, with the only possible pathway filled with timber, small and large, crossed and crisscrossed; and now, while the horses and mules are feeding on innutritious wire grass, you will not wonder at 'only sixteen miles a day.'

'Didn't the hostile Indians go there?' the reader inquires. Yes; they jammed their ponies through, up the rocks, over, and under, and around the logs and among the fallen trees, without attempting to cut a limb, leaving blood to mark their path; and abandoned animals, with broken legs, or played out, or stretched dead by the wayside.

Sixteen years have elapsed since the Nez Perce outbreak, and the Lolo Trail, becoming yearly more and more obstructed, exists now only in history, for it is almost obliterated and practically abandoned. The region it traversed has relapsed again into its primitive state—a vast unbroken wilderness, thrillingly interesting in its history and traditions and impressively beautiful in its bold, majestic scenery. Far removed from the outposts of civilization; the watercourses impracticable for boats or canoes; and the region practically inaccessible except by the difficult Lolo Trail—the basin of the Clearwater River, with its vast forests, dense thickets, and innumerable streams, will remain for many years to come a natural and ideal home for large game—a safe and quiet retreat—a haven where the native denizens of the forest need have no fear of molestation.

Chapter II

The Equipment

"It's a 'bird,' and fits me exactly," said Will, referring to his new gun, as soon as the usual handshaking and salutations were over, "and I want you to come right up to our room and see it."

"Wait until you see mine, old man," replied Abe, who had just arrived in Spokane from the East to join Will's hunting party. "It is the best all-around, general-service gun I ever saw," continued Abe, "but let me arrange to have my baggage sent up."

In a half-hour the two intimates were comfortably settled in a large room of Hotel Spokane and were admiring their guns, which had been built especially for the trip.

Will's gun was a three-barreled paradox, weight under eight pounds, and had been completed only a few weeks previously by one of the leading gunmakers in the country. It had two 12-gauge barrels side by side, paradox-bored (rifled for a few inches in the muzzle, so as to shoot balls accurately), and a 32-calibre rifle-barrel directly underneath the shot-barrels. The rifle-barrel was chambered for the popular 32-40-165 Winchester cartridge, while the shot-barrels took the standard 2 7/8-inch paper shell. Will had given a carte blanche order for the very best material and workmanship, and the gunmaker had exhausted all of Will's patience by consuming fourteen months in its production. But it was a beauty! Balance excellent; locks that worked smoothly and silk-like; the stock the finest Italian walnut; while the workmanship, the lines, fitting, and engraving were simply superb.

Abe's gun was an ordinary 12-gauge Winchester repeating shotgun into which a paradox-barrel had been fitted, thus converting it into a repeating rifle as well. Both guns were unique, and had been evolved by the two "gun cranks" during the preceding two years. Besides shooting ball, both guns could handle shot and buckshot about as well as the average cylinder-bored guns of the same gauge.

"Let me see one of your ball cartridges," said Abe.

"Here's one I cut open yesterday," said Will, producing an ordinary A-grade paper shell, slit its whole length longitudinally and exposing a conical bullet with one groove. Five wads separated the bullet and powder.

"Odd-shaped bullet, isn't it?" said Abe. "But what results were gotten shooting alternate barrels at two hundred yards?"—referring to a test the gunmaker had agreed to make.

Will unrolled a large pasteboard target, showing ten shots which had been fired consecutively with alternate barrels at a distance of two hundred yards. The shots were all on a circle eleven and three-quarter inches in diameter, and well bunched in and around an eight-inch bull's-eye.

"Jove, why that's as good as the average hunting rifle will do!" exclaimed Abe. "I thought I would surprise you with the test score of my gun, but yours is just as good, if not better. We never dreamed of getting results like this, did we?"

"It knocks out anything they have ever accomplished in Europe with paradox guns," replied Will.

"The old man evidently knew what he was talking about when he guaranteed to turn out as good paradox-barrels as could be obtained anywhere, although I admit I doubted his ability to do so at the time. But now, what about the trip?" asked Abe.

"Well, I had the hardest time you ever heard of getting reliable information about the game here, but one thing is certain: It is too late to hunt mountain sheep, unless you want to take your chances of getting snowed in. The best trip we can take under the circumstances, so far as I can judge, is to go to the headwaters of the Clearwater in eastern Idaho. A guide I was talking with yesterday guaranteed us shots at elk and says if not too late we will be sure to get bear there too. He says that there are any quantity of blacktail deer, a few moose, and on the high peaks goats, but that it is too late to go up to the peaks this fall. How would that kind of a trip suit you?"

"You know, Will, that I had set my heart on getting a bighorn," replied Abe. "But if that is out of the question, I'm perfectly satisfied with the trip to the Clearwater country if you are. What have you done about an outfit?"

"Almost nothing. The character of the outfit depends largely upon where we expect to go, and so I had to wait for you. You remember our old cook, Colgate? Well, he is ready to start on a moment's notice. I had him go up to the St. Joe country to see about getting bear dogs, and Palmer kindly sent two of his down yesterday with this note." Here Will handed Abe a note reading as follows:

Dear Carlin:

I send you two terrier dogs, which we have used with success on bear, etc., on condition that you come up and pay us a visit on your return. Hoping they may be of service to you, I am most cordially yours,

Fred Palmer.

"Fred is a good one, isn't he?" said Abe, returning the letter. "We're awfully lucky to get those dogs. We'll have a great hunt yet."

Just then the door opened, and John, the third member of the party, came in. After a few minutes of conversation, Will and Abe went out to see the guide, while John busied himself with some correspondence.

The guide, Martin Spencer, was soon found, and satisfactory arrangements were made with him to guide the party. The three then returned to the hotel to prepare a list of the provisions and camping paraphernalia required for a five-weeks' trip. Colgate had arrived in the meantime, and he and Spencer prepared the following list of provisions:

125 lbs. flour	30 lbs. sugar
30 lbs. breakfast bacon	1 lb. tea
40 lbs. salt pork	8 lbs. coffee
20 lbs. beans	2 doz. cans cond. milk
40 lbs. salt	3 lbs. baking powder
10 lbs. oatmeal	citron, sage, mace, thyme
10 lbs. cornmeal	10 lbs. alum

5 lbs. dried apples	5 lbs. raisins
5 lbs. dried apricots	1/2 lb. pepper
1 gal. maple syrup	1/2 gal. vinegar
2 doz. tallow candles	block matches
3 lbs. laundry soap	1 gal. brandy
1/2 doz. cakes toilet soap	40 lbs. potatoes

Spencer, Will and Abe prepared the following list of camp equipage:

1 10x12 ft. wall tent	1/2 doz. knives and forks
1 7x7 ft. A-tent	9 tin plates
1 large wagon cover or fly	9 tin cups
10 double blankets	1/2 doz. teaspoons
2 heavy quilts	2 butcher's knives
1/2 doz. towels	2 large spoons
3 canvas pack covers 4x6	1 large meat knife
5 yds. crash	1 4-lb. axe
5 yds. heavy unbleached muslin	1 2-lb. axe
3 camp kettles (nested)	1 8-in. flat file
2 gold plans for use as dishpans, etc.	1 box assorted copper-wire rivets
1 granite stew pan	2 10-yard coils wire
2 frying pans	2 lbs. assorted wire nails
1 reflector (for baking bread)	1 ball coarse twine
1 coffee pot	1 ball light twine
	50 ft. extra rope
	1 rubber airbed
	1 doz extra cloth sacks

In addition to the guns already mentioned, Spencer took a 40-70-330 Winchester single-shot rifle with reloading tools and plenty of ammunition. John's arms consisted of a 45-90-300 Winchester repeating rifle and a Schofield model Smith & Wesson revolver. Will and Abe both had Smith & Wesson Russian model revolvers. A 40-82-260 Winchester repeating rifle was taken as a reserve gun in case any of the other guns should break down or be in any way disabled on the trip. The whole party was well supplied with fishing tackle. Will had an Eastman folding camera with all modern improvements and fitted with an excellent lens. Abe took one of the new "Trokonets," a hand camera, for which a harness had been made so it could be carried on his back. A screwdriver to take apart guns, gun oil, toilet cases, sewing materials, hunting knives, tobacco, etc., completed the camp furniture and supplies. Unfortunately, by an oversight, Mr. Palmer had failed to send us the names of the two terriers, and as it was impossible to communicate with him before starting into the woods, the two dogs were named "Idaho" and "Montana"—the names being suggested by the proximity of our proposed hunting ground to the boundary line between those states. A fine spaniel belonging to Colgate was also taken with us for grouse.

Spencer estimated that five packhorses would be necessary to carry the provisions and, as there were five persons in the party, five saddle horses with complete trappings were also required. The following day Spencer and Will were delegated to purchase the horses, trappings, etc., Abe to buy the camp equipage, while Colgate attended to the purchase of the groceries and provisions.

In the matter of food, only necessaries were taken, the object being to avoid excessive weight. All the provisions were done up in cloth sacks, to avoid the danger of spilling or losing them. A rail car had been chartered in the meantime, into which the whole equipment was loaded as fast as purchased. Early the following morning the car left for Kendrick, Idaho, the nearest railway station to the Clearwater country. The party followed an hour later in the passenger train, arriving at Kendrick late in the afternoon. On the arrival of the freight train that evening, the horses were removed from the car to a small enclosure or corral near the railroad siding and fed. The safety of the balance of the things left in the car was next attended to, after which the party found comfortable accommodations for the night at the St. Elmo Hotel.

Chapter III

On the Lolo Trail

Suitable arrangements having been made the preceding evening, at dawn on the morning of September 18th a number of the horses were taken to the blacksmith shop to be shod. While that operation was in progress, all the camp equipage and provisions were arranged into packages of convenient form and weight, called "packs," and lashed to the horses as fast as they were shod. At one o'clock of the same day all the final preparations were completed and the caravan—or "outfit," to use the western term—started for the mountains. The whole party was in excellent spirits, and the easy fourteen-mile ride to Snell's mill, through a rolling farming country, was very much enjoyed. We halted just at sundown. Supper was soon ready and was partaken of with much relish by the light of the campfire. Mr. Snell kindly gave us permission to sleep in his barn, and all passed a comfortable night with newly mown hay for a bed.

The next day we started off bright and early. The Nez Perce Indian Reservation was entered before noon. A few hours later the party crossed the North Fork of the Clearwater on a ferryboat operated by Indians. From the North Fork the route led along the Clearwater River for several miles and then ascended the high mountain on the north side of the river. Camp was made near the summit at about four o'clock in the afternoon. After the packs and saddles had been removed from the horses, Abe started out with Daisy for some grouse and returned in about an hour with three, which were prepared for supper.

The following morning, September 20th, was cloudy, and several light showers during the forenoon made the riding very disagreeable. At noon the party reached Weippe, where forty pounds of potatoes were purchased from Mr. Gafney. The journey was then resumed through open glades and strips of timber to Brown's Creek. Here an old cabin furnished excellent shelter, as it was raining when the party arrived there. Will and Abe killed several grouse during the day, which were enjoyed at the evening meal.

At Brown's Creek

The next morning it was raining hard. Consequently, we decided to remain at the cabin that day. In the middle of the forenoon, however, Will and Abe became impatient. The former got his fly book and said he was going to try the trout in the little brook, and the latter took his gun to see if any grouse could be found. John also sallied out in quest of grouse, taking his revolver. In about an hour's time Will returned to the cabin with fifty-three trout, a quarter-pound to one and a half pounds in weight, and reported rare sport in taking them. The stream was so small that he had cut a willow switch about seven feet long and, with only four feet of line, had been able to take in an hour all we could use. Abe and John returned to the cabin at noon with only two grouse each.

That afternoon a man who had come over to Brown's Creek to drive out some cattle called at our camp. He was a typical mountain rancher, wearing a slicker and chaps and a large wide-brimmed hat. On his pony, or "cayuse," he carried a week's supply of provisions, a gun, and an axe. Hitching his cayuse to the fence, he approached the cabin. Seeing Spencer, who was outside at the time, he addressed him.

"Hello, pardner. You struck a pretty good camp here on a rainy day, didn't yez?"

Spencer, surmising the man to be the possible owner of the cabin, was very polite and explained the situation and the circumstances which led to our taking possession of the cabin.

The rancher then continued, "Oh, you fellers is all right. I reckon if the owner of the cabin was here, he'd make you go inter the new cabin yander. But say, hain't you the man what took an outfit into the mountains last fall?"

Spencer replied that he had taken a party last fall over the same route we were traveling and stated about the time they had passed through there.

"I tho't I'd seed you afore," said the rancher, and then he related the circumstances, which Spencer remembered. This put them on the ground of old acquaintances, and after a few minutes' conversation relative to the last year's trip, the rancher stated, "I reckon you'll have a hard time in the snow so late in the fall."

"We got out last year all right as late as the 20th of October," said Spencer, "and we figure on getting out this time by the 15th."

"It's a pretty tough trip for tenderfeet," the rancher continued. "Do you fellers all think you can stand the trip?" he asked, turning toward Will and assuming that the whole party except the guide were unused to the woods.

"Oh, I think we'll pull through all right," said Will, who then directed the conversation to the subject of hunting. The various kinds of game and the best places in the region were discussed for a half hour or more, whereupon the rancher departed, accepting the dozen trout which Will offered him.

At about ten o'clock of September 22nd, we crossed Musselshell Creek. Up to this time the route had been along a wagon road through a sparsely timbered and rolling country, and the traveling was comparatively easy. Here, however, was the terminus of the wagon road. Forming in single file, with Spencer in the lead, the pack animals were distributed between the riders, and the train continued the journey eastward into the mountains along the Lolo Trail.

The character of the country soon changed. The trail led up a steep ascent, passing through dense growths of timber. At about three o'clock we reached the top of a high ridge called Snow Summit. Here we found six inches of snow on the ground. Proceeding a little farther, we turned abruptly to the right and, descending into a neighboring ravine, we came to a glade with a little brook, where we made camp.

Making Camp at Snow Summit

The snow was about eight inches deep, but directly around the base of a large cedar at one side of the glade the snow had disappeared. On this limited area of bare ground we piled our gear and set about preparing supper. Although we had not come prepared for winter weather, there was a bountiful supply of blankets and plenty of excellent firewood near at hand, so the night was passed without discomfort.

The next day's ride was very difficult and tedious. The trail, besides being steep and crooked, was obstructed by hundreds of fallen trees. Some of these the horses could step over, others they would jump, while those that were too high had to be flanked. In the latter case, it was always necessary to leave the train, and it was often extremely difficult to get the horses through the dense brush and tangled fallen timber which surrounded these obstructions. Usually the packtrain would follow the leader without much difficulty, but occasionally they would wander off and get wound up in the brush and fallen timber so badly and act so stupidly that the language which the man who rounded them up invariably used was entirely justified.

About two o'clock we reached a glade four miles from Rocky Ridge, where two small streams rise and flow in opposite directions. As it was a journey of five hours to the next desirable camping place, Spencer decided to make camp at this point. Although three to five inches of snow covered the ground, a space of bare ground was found on the west side of the glade near several large trees, where a camp was soon established. With camp made, Will went fishing and caught a mess of nice trout in a short time. Will and Abe then went down one stream, while John descended the other for a few hours' hunt. The bag was eight grouse which, with those killed during the day along the trail, swelled the aggregate to seventeen.

The following day, September 24th, was the hardest day we experienced until we reached our destination. The trail zigzagged up and down steep hillsides, crossed rocky gulches, and skirted or "cross-cutted" steep slopes of loose rock. Occasionally the horses would refuse to go, and it became necessary to dismount and lead and drive them. Sometimes a horse would step into an opening between the rocks and get stuck, so that he had to be backed in order that he might release himself. The horses' legs became so badly scratched and bruised that they left bloodmarks in the snow. About noon we arrived at a small stream which had eroded a steep narrow gulch in the side of the mountain. The trail at that point was so rough and uneven that the horses could find no comfortable place to stand, and they became very restless during the ten minutes that we halted to water them and eat our hasty midday lunch. In the afternoon the trail led along steep, open hillsides covered with loose rock, permitting occasionally extended views of the surrounding country. That night we reached and camped on Bald Mountain.

On the Trail to Bald Mountain

On the maps of this region Bald Mountain is represented as a single, isolated peak. It actually belongs to and forms part of a mountain range. Towering considerably above the surrounding ranges and peaks, with about three-quarters of its top destitute of timber and often covered with snow, it is very conspicuous and forms a convenient and unmistakable landmark. Before darkness came on, Will, Abe, John, and Spencer walked to its summit to take a look at the surrounding region, and they were amply rewarded. To the north and northwest, spread out before them like an immense map—save that the streams lay hidden deep in their eroded canyons—were the entire basins of the St. Joseph and St. Mary Rivers, while in the more immediate vicinity could be plainly distinguished the basin of the North Fork of the Clearwater. To the south and west were the basins of three other main forks of the Clearwater

River. On the east, extending almost from the north to the south and covered with snow, was the main range of the Bitterroot Mountains boldly outlined against the sky; far off to the south could be seen five of the "Seven Devils," while away in the hazy southwestern horizon were dimly discerned the Blue Mountains of Oregon. Between all these and Bald Mountain, rising to greater or less altitudes, many of them fringed with snow, were an infinite number of ranges, no doubt towering high above the intervening valleys but dwarfed into insignificance when viewed from Bald Mountain.

We had made our camp near a large, solitary fir tree, under which we expected to sleep, for the night was clear and it was thought unnecessary to go to the trouble of pitching a tent. It had been our custom after removing the packs and saddles from the horses to hobble one or two of them and let the others run disencumbered. On this occasion Spencer picketed his powerful white horse with a rope about thirty feet long, tying the end of the rope to a stump. After supper it was quite dark, and all were gathered around the fire. Suddenly a loud tramping was heard, and our hearts almost stopped beating at the thought that the horses had stampeded. Then Spencer's white horse rushed out of the darkness, passed within thirty feet of the camp-fire, and tore at breakneck speed straight down the steep mountainside into the gloom and darkness below, a piece of the stump skipping and bounding after him at the end of the rope. In a moment all was still. In the excitement we had imagined the stump to be a cougar in pursuit of the horse, and Will had grabbed his gun to shoot it. Will and Spencer immediately started down the mountain to see what had become of the horse. In about fifteen minutes they returned and reported him safe and sound. He had succeeded in tearing loose from the stump and miraculously escaped a violent death. Fortunately none of the other horses stampeded, and congratulations were in order on our good fortune in avoiding a stampede, as well as for the opportunity of witnessing the fastest time ever made down so steep an incline. It was a spectacle that will never be forgotten by those who saw it.

The day following—September 25th—the trail led along the high crest of the main divide between the Kooskooskee and the North Fork of the Clearwater. A great many bear and deer and several elk tracks were noted as we journeyed along in the snow. The elevated position of the trail as we passed from one side to the other of the divide afforded us magnificent views of our surroundings, and the scenery was much enjoyed. From time to time Spencer would point out landmarks and places of interest to the hunters. That evening the Indian "post offices" were reached (two piles of stones several feet high on each side of the trail). Turning to the right at that point, we descended about five hundred feet into a gulch and camped for the night near a spring.

On the Divide

Returning to the trail the next morning, we followed it only a short distance and then turned to the right and took an old Indian trail leading along a burnt ridge down to the

Kooskooskee [Lochsa River]. The last portion of the descent was very steep, the trail zigzagging down the nose of a spur, the altitude of which was at least three thousand feet above the river. During this descent Colgate became exhausted, and Will dismounted and assisted him down. On our arrival at the foot of the descent, Colgate's feet and legs were found to be considerably swollen. His condition alarmed Will very much, and on inquiring into the cause of the swelling and his weakness, Colgate insisted he was simply tired out and would be all right in a day or two after having a little rest.

On reaching the river, all were surprised to find a cabin nearly completed and four men encamped. Spencer went over to the camp and soon returned with the information that a prospector whom he had known for years, named Jerry Johnson, and a trapper, Ben Keeley, had built the cabin in partnership, packed in plenty of grub from Missoula, and were going to spend the winter there. The other two men had come in for a few days' hunting and would return shortly to Missoula.

Chapter IV

The Lost Indian Prospect

Six feet in height, with a powerful frame slightly bent by advancing years, black hair mixed with gray, jet black eyes, and a stubbly gray beard—Jerry Johnson, the prospector, would arouse curiosity and interest anywhere.

A Prussian by birth, Johnson emigrated at an early age to New Zealand. There he became interested in mining, and since then he has devoted his life to prospecting for the precious metals in the wildest and most unfrequented regions of the earth, occasionally acting in the capacity of guide, hunter, and packer. Enthusiastically devoted to his work and often with no other companion than his faithful dog, he has carried pole-pick, axe and gun and clambered over the mountains under all conditions of weather and climate. For fifteen years he has searched for gold in the most inaccessible regions of the Cascades and the Rocky Mountains, and now, at the advanced age of sixty years, rugged from hardship and exposure, he still loves the isolation and solitude of the mountains and is seeking with characteristic perseverance the long lost Indian Prospect.

Many years ago, while Johnson was encamped in the heart of the Bitterroot Mountains, a half-starved Indian found his way to Johnson's camp. The Indian was given food and shelter. Grateful for the favors shown him, in broken English and by signs and gestures he informed Johnson that he knew where there was "Heap Elk City, heap Pierce City"—meaning much gold, there being mines at the places named. Johnson at once engaged the Indian to guide him to the place. Returning to the nearest point where supplies could be purchased, he secured an adequate equipment, and with one other man and the Indian started back into the mountains.

Jerry Johnson

The route taken by the Indian was along the Lolo Trail to the Warm Springs. Here the Indian fell sick, but the party pushed on fifteen miles farther east to a small prairie which Johnson calls "The Park." When they reached this point, the Indian became so sick that he could proceed no farther. Fearing he might die, Johnson got the Indian to tell him how the gold was found. This was quite difficult, as the Indian could speak but a few words of English and had to convey most of the information by gestures. The story he told was substantially as follows:

Some years previously a party of Indians were encamped at the place Johnson was seeking and one of them became very sick. A sweat bath was thus prepared for him. While preparing this sweat bath, it was necessary to loosen and remove some white rock, and while doing this the Indians discovered that the rock was full of gold or, as the Indian called it, "Elk City."

The Indian guide grew worse and weaker every hour, and Johnson, being alarmed, took him in his arms and carried him to a more elevated position where a view to the eastward could be obtained.

"Which way from here?" asked Johnson.

With his remaining strength, the Indian raised his arm and pointed to a peak covered with snow. "See snow?" he replied. Raising one finger, he pronounced the single word "sun," and rolled over on his blanket exhausted. A few hours later he died.

Not discouraged by his ill fortune, Johnson and his companion buried the Indian and pushed on to the peak indicated by him and searched the country beyond and surrounding the peak all that summer, but never succeeded in finding the old Indian camp. Since that time he has spent several summers fruitlessly in the same neighborhood and is now passing the winter in that desolate, snowbound region, hoping early in the spring to continue his search for the Lost Indian Prospect.

Chapter V

In Camp

On the north bank of the Kooskooskee, at the edge of a flat or bottom a quarter of a mile in length and averaging a couple of hundred yards in width, we made our camp in the midst of a young growth of pine and fir trees. At our feet rushed the clear, foaming, roaring waters of the river; all around us towered the awful mountains, rising to altitudes of from two to four thousand feet above the river, many of them covered with snow and glistening in the bright sunlight. It was a beautiful spot.

But time was precious, and much as we admired our surroundings, we soon gave our attention to matters more practical. The packs were immediately taken from the horses, the saddles removed, and those animals having sore backs had their wounds treated by a healing wash of alum water. Those likely to stray off were hobbled and turned loose, and then all hands set to work to make camp comfortable. Spencer and Abe put up the wall tent and fly and got our gear under shelter, while the rest busied themselves in unpacking and preparing a meal. After dinner a supply of firewood was secured, several fir trees were felled and the twigs and needles trimmed from them for beds. A rude table was constructed under the fly, and before darkness came on we were arranging a program for the morrow.

Spencer was to guide us to the lower warm springs the following morning, so we rose before daybreak. We ate a hearty breakfast, and although it rained, we sallied out just at dawn. A good trail followed along the bank of the river and the hillside, but it was overgrown with brush which hung, dripping, over it. We were wet to the skin long before we reached the springs, but we kept cheerfully on. When near the springs, Spencer took the lead, with Will close behind. We approached too rapidly, however, and a deer which had been at the springs to lick was scared away before any of us could get a shot.

Spencer gave us some general information concerning the country for a few miles around to aid us in our future hunting. After walking a mile farther down the river, we returned to camp, wet and bedraggled, in time for dinner.

In the afternoon Spencer took Will and Abe to the upper warm springs, three miles above camp. As these springs were on the other side of the river, three horses were caught and saddled. Will and Abe expected to stay all night, so blankets and a day's provisions were taken along.

Unfortunately, it continued to rain. After showing them the springs and helping them take care of the horses for the night, Spencer made some valuable suggestions relative to the habits of the game in that locality and returned to the main camp. Will and Abe made a temporary camp under a large white cedar. They saw plenty of fresh tracks and were pleased at the outlook for a successful hunt, but it rained all night, and since they could not keep dry or comfortable without a tent, they returned to the main camp about noon the next day.

A Meal in Camp

Colgate was now a trifle improved but not strong enough to attend to his duties. We all thus helped do the cooking and the work about camp.

Day after day it rained, the sky never once clearing off. We knew we could not stay long in any case, so we were compelled to make the best of it and hunted every day in the rain. As we became more familiar with the locality and the habits of the game, we met with fair success, but the rain interfered greatly with the pleasure of hunting, and the raw, cold air was very uncomfortable. Hunting under these conditions always involved a thorough wetting as well as the necessity of moving about in order to maintain proper circulation of the blood and avoid taking colds. Much of the time in camp, especially in the evenings, was devoted to the drying of our wet clothing. The blankets were always damp, and we frequently held them up to the fire before retiring for the night. An adequate supply of firewood was usually brought in before dark, at the expense of considerable labor, but with a large, blazing campfire and congenial companions, all discomforts were forgotten and we invariably fell asleep indulging the deluded hope that the next day would be fair. John, who seemed to be more sensitive to the cold than the rest of the party, did not care to suffer as much exposure and consequently hunted very little. He was, besides, particularly unfortunate. On one occasion he was within range of a large band of elk but lost a shot at them by an accident. At another time he was walking along the trail without a gun and came suddenly on a bear. He was, however, very successful with smaller game, of which he bagged a large quantity.

Chapter VI

The First Elk

We had been in camp for over five days and had as yet not been fortunate enough to secure any fresh meat. It had rained every day. The game moved about but little and visited the licks and their drinking places at night. Will, who was the most experienced hunter of the party, felt assured of this fact, for he had hunted at all times of the day about the springs, and while there were fresh signs, they had evidently been made the night before. On the evening of the fifth day, fresh elk sign was seen along the hillsides, and we felt pretty certain that the elk had either commenced coming down from the high ranges or that those already in our vicinity had begun to move about regardless of the wet weather. Accordingly, Will determined to visit the lower lick at daylight the following morning and spend the day in hunting the adjacent sidehills.

He started for the lower lick just at dawn and returned to camp at about eleven o'clock carrying a large heart in his hand. The others had been busy all morning making camp more comfortable, but as soon as Will was seen approaching, every one became at once deeply interested and came forward to meet him.

"Well, what is it?" asked Abe.

"Bull elk," said Will, laconically.

"The devil!" said Abe, taking Will's hand and giving it a warm squeeze of congratulation. "Luck at last, and fresh meat in camp!"

After congratulations all around, Will went into the tent, laid his rifle on the blankets, and began to change his wet clothes.

"But tell us something about it. Has he a nice set of horns?" asked John.

"Six points and full grown," said Will briefly, adding, "Say, out there, I want you people to know I'm hungry!"

A hasty meal had been prepared by the time Will had changed clothes and hung them on a line near the fire. Seating himself at the table, he gave the following account of his morning's experience:

"As it was raining when I started, and considering the chances of seeing game very slim, I decided to take the 40-82 instead of my paradox. I started on a rapid walk for the lower lick, but the brush along the trail was sopping wet and I got wet to the skin before going half a mile. On arriving at the grove of cedars in which the spring is situated, I used the utmost caution in approaching the lick, but found it empty. As I stood debating a moment what I should do, I heard the clear whistle of a cow, which I judged must be about a hundred and fifty yards below me on a small flat skirting the river. Slipping quietly along the brow of the hill, I had hardly emerged from the timber when the cow trotted slowly past me, not more than thirty yards away, without seeming in the least disturbed by my presence. Hastily getting behind a large tree, I waited for the bull, which I felt confident would follow her. I had not been there more than half a minute when I saw a pair of magnificent antlers moving slowly from right to left in front of me. The head and body were hidden from view, as the bull was walking up a little gully eighty yards away. I did not dare move, for a few jumps would take the bull out of sight in the timber. Although I did not stir, and he could not possibly have scented me, the bull seemed aware that there was some danger at hand. He suddenly sprang up the side of the gully, stopped in an open clump of trees, and stood as though trying to decide in what direction the danger lay. His neck and shoulders were hidden by intervening trees, but I felt that I must make the best of the shot offered me and aimed for the liver. At the report of the rifle he gave one bound and disappeared over the brow of the hill. Hastening to the spot, I found his tracks following a well-worn game trail which led, slanting, down the hill. There were no signs of blood, but I felt sure that I had hit him. Walking with extreme caution and peering into all the little ravines and thickets, I had gone about half a mile when, on stooping down and glancing ahead, I saw the elk lying behind a log seventy-five yards distant and looking directly at me.

"Sitting down quietly, I took careful aim at his neck and fired. The elk staggered to his feet and made for the river. Hastily throwing down the lever and inserting a fresh cartridge, I fired for his shoulder. At the shot he went down on his chest, but regained his feet and started off on three legs. The next shot struck him in the neck, and he went down all in a heap. He was not dead, however, and for fear that he might break his antlers on the rocks in his struggles, I finished him with a shot in the neck. My first sensation was a feeling of great satisfaction at killing the finest elk that I had ever seen; my second was a feeling of disgust with the gun for doing it in such a bungling manner. One shot from a proper rifle in the neck or shoulder, where these miserable little hollow-pointed bullets had struck, would have killed him outright. For full five minutes I sat and admired the fallen monarch: his magnificent curving antlers; his splendid form and sleek, yellowish sides; the fine, long, reddish-black hair of his scalp and neck. Then, on preparing to bleed and dress him, I found that I had forgotten my long-bladed knife in my haste to get away early this morning and had only a large pocketknife with me. With this, however, I dressed the elk and hastened back to camp."

After congratulations a second time, we all went down with horses to bring up the meat and antlers. Keeley accompanied us to get some fresh meat, of which he and Jerry were in need. On our arrival we found the usual number of magpies and ravens rapidly making away with the entrails amid a perfect pandemonium of harsh sounds. When they saw us, they flew into neighboring trees and watched our proceedings.

After photographing the elk, we skinned and cut him up, and at four o'clock we were ready to start back to camp. The first bullet had cut his liver almost in two and had lodged under the skin on the other side. The second bullet had barely broken one shoulder and smashed into bits on the big bones, failing to penetrate farther. None of the last three bullets had passed through the neck, which was very thick even for this season of the year.

We started for camp and were overtaken by darkness half a mile beyond the lick. Keeley's horse slipped and rolled down a slippery sidehill, but by dint of considerable swearing and work on the part of his master, the horse was brought back to the trail. The darkness became so intense when a mile from camp that we were forced to build a fire, unpack the horses, and leave the meat and antlers under a tree till morning. While the fire was being built, one of the horses clumsily struck a dead tree, about eight inches in diameter. The tree fell and just grazed Will's arm—a very fortunate escape from a broken shoulder.

All the matches were used in trying to start the fire, and we had a miserable time stumbling about in the darkness. After we had floundered around for an hour or so, Keeley came along with a torch made from cedar shavings, and we reached camp about eight o'clock. It took us four hours to go less than four miles. We secured the meat and antlers the first thing the next morning.

Chapter VII

A Hunt at the Upper Warm Springs

It had been raining all morning and Abe, thoroughly drenched, had just returned from a hunt at the lower lick. He had seen nothing and looked a trifle disappointed.

"Let's go to the upper lick and stay all night," said Will. "The moon is down at nights now, and there ought to be a good show mornings and evenings."

"I'll go with you," said Abe. "As soon as I get on dry things, we'll hunt up the horses."

The horses were found grazing on the side of the ridge above the flat, and two of them were soon caught, brought in, and saddled. A double blanket each; a small camp kettle, inside of which were packed two tin cups, two spoons, two tin plates, and a small quantity of salt, coffee, sugar, condensed milk, and bacon; some raw elk steak, bread, a hand axe, and some ropes—all were suitably arranged and fastened to the horses. At two o'clock we were ready to start.

The trail led up the riverbank and for a quarter of a mile was lined on both sides by bushes loaded with berries. A little farther on, the steep slopes of two rocky points were passed, where the trail was so rough that we dismounted and led the horses along with great difficulty.

When we reached the ford, a mile above camp, the river was found to be much higher than when we forded it before. We ventured into it, however, and although the current almost swept the horses off their feet and sometimes reached halfway up their sides, with the combined weight of ourselves and the packs on their backs, they managed to keep their footing and carried us safely across. The river at this point is about a hundred yards wide, and a large creek empties into it from the east, which has formed a flat of several acres near its mouth. The trail crosses the flat and follows the creek. Occasionally it was necessary to climb over high ledges that projected into the creek, jump fallen trees, force our way through thickets of fir and pine. In three-quarters of an hour we reached a point a mile and a half from the river and half a mile from the springs, where we decided to camp. We selected a suitable spot near plenty of firewood, the horses were unsaddled, and the gear placed under leaning cedars where it would remain dry until a shelter was built. While Abe took the horses back to the flat on the river and picketed them in good bunchgrass, Will propped up a small pole horizontally about five feet above the ground and as far ahead of and parallel to a large log lying on the ground. Limbs and saplings long enough to span across were then placed at intervals, their ends resting on the pole and log. Smaller limbs were then spread on crosswise, and the whole covered thickly with small branches and needles of fir and pine. A sloping roof was thus built, which shed a slow rain very satisfactorily.

When Abe returned, the shelter was almost finished, requiring only a few more fir needles for the roof. A hasty glance was taken to note the dry timber. The blankets and provisions were placed under the shelter, the guns and ammunition inspected, and everything being found in good condition, we continued on foot up the trail. Directly we came to a small warm spring issuing from the face of a boulder forty feet high and discharging its water in three or four separate streams. The steam rose in a column high in the air. Following the trail, we passed over the boulder near its face and in close proximity to the steam. A quarter of a mile farther on, just before getting in sight of the first of the larger springs, the trail makes a steep descent through a thicket of fir and pine saplings. Our acrobatic accomplishments were here brought into requisition, for had we walked down in the usual way, any game at the spring would have seen our feet before we could even have seen out of the thicket.

"You go ahead," said Will, Abe not yet having had a shot at an elk.

"All right," answered Abe, and disregarding the wet and the mud, Abe got down on all fours, with his head close to the ground, and gradually crept down toward the opening at the foot of the descent. He took fully two minutes to go the last twenty feet. On reaching the bottom, he beckoned Will to follow as there was nothing in the lick.

After leaving the thicket, the trail passes through a small glade or opening in the timber, about two acres in area. This opening slopes gradually toward the creek, which forms its right hand edge or boundary. In the center of the opening, issuing from beneath a bunch of boulders, is the main spring, which, with other smaller springs, spreads its waters over an acre or so of stones and pebbles between the source of the springs and the creek, coating them with a white saline deposit which forms the lick and attracts the game. The remainder of the opening is covered with a luxuriant growth of grass. At all times, and especially in cold weather, the steam from the spring rises in great clouds, although the water is not so hot but that one can easily retain the hand in it.

A dense grove of white cedars, firs, and pines, one hundred and fifty yards in width, separates these springs from several other large springs higher up the creek, which are similarly located in an opening several acres in extent.

By the time the grove was reached it was four o'clock, and it was decided Abe should take the upper lick and Will the lower one. Since the wind was moving toward the grove across the upper lick, Abe took his stand on the leeward side in the deep shade of the grove behind two fir trees. Will took a similar position near the lick below.

Save for the roaring of the creek, everything remained quiet and motionless. Finally darkness came on. Abe was just beginning to think of going back to Will and then returning to camp, for he could no longer see the sights of his gun. Suddenly a twig snapped directly behind him, and Abe turned his head, thinking Will had come over to see if he was ready to return to camp. Seeing nothing in the dense gloom, however, Abe imagined the alarm to have been caused by some natural means and gave his whole attention to the lick again.

Imagine his surprise when, about three minutes later, he was startled by an angry snort and a savage growl behind him. Abe's first instinct was, of course, to shoot, and wheeling around he saw a large grizzly bear within fifteen feet of him, just entering the lick. His gun was pointed at the bear and his finger was pressing the trigger when he observed two cubs following the bear. Discretion instantaneously arrested the pressure on the trigger. After the bear got into the lick and was at least twenty yards distant, Abe fired two shots at her, aiming roughly along his gun barrel. Both shots missed. Abe then ran out into the open lick, where it was lighter, and fired a third shot just as the bear was about to enter the forest on the other side of the lick. At the report, the bear raised on its haunches, turned back toward Abe, and pawed the air frantically. Now was his chance. Abe aimed as carefully as he could over the top of the barrel, but the gun snapped. There were only three cartridges in the magazine. Before he could reload, the bear and cubs had disappeared in the woods on the opposite side of the lick. Just then Will came running up, all out of breath.

"What are you shooting at?" he asked.

Abe was so badly disappointed and disgusted that he failed to answer him at once. Finally he said, "Just think! A grizzly and two cubs! They came up behind me, passed within fifteen feet of me, crossed the lick, and, by thunder, got away from me! If it had been fifteen minutes earlier, I could have seen my sights and I'd have had the whole crowd. Why, the cubs would have weighed a hundred pounds apiece!"

"Which way did they go?" asked Will anxiously.

"Right out here—but look where the old one tore up the earth at the third shot!" said Abe, pointing to the tracks where the bear was when he wounded her.

"You hit her then! Is there no blood on the trail? What's the matter with following?" asked Will.

"It's too dark to see blood," said Abe, "and besides, it's dangerous to follow at night. We'll have to wait until morning."

Abe then took Will to the stand he had occupied and told him all the details, concluding with, "What I can't understand is why the bear should approach me when the wind blew from me directly toward her. She must have scented me all the while."

"She was probably looking for a meal for the cubs," said Will. "They must have crossed the creek too."

"Well, I'll admit it was a 'startler,' for I wasn't looking for game from that quarter, but I'm glad I did not shoot when I first saw her."

Both Will and Abe were almost sick from disappointment and deplored the hard luck all the way back to camp.

It was now quite dark and the rain began to fall faster. Arriving at the shelter, they soon had a fire going with the aid of a little pitch pine. Will had brought up water from the creek, and while that was boiling, the steak was fried in the lid of the bucket and some fried potatoes warmed up in a plate. In twenty minutes we had excellent coffee, and in twenty more had partaken of a very satisfactory meal.

We then pulled down some dry stubs which, with some fallen limbs, furnished firewood for the night. Taking turns, we each kept up the fire half the night and managed to pass it quite comfortably.

The next morning we had breakfast and were on our stands at the licks before daylight. Nothing appearing by eight o'clock, Will went over to Abe, and the search for the bear and cubs was immediately begun. Crossing the lick, the tracks in the soft mud and pebbles were very plain, but on entering the woods it was found that the rain during the night had washed away every trace of the retreating bears. We then decided to follow up the creek bottom some distance, in a sort of general search, keeping about fifty yards apart. We had proceeded only a few hundred yards when Will fired two shots in rapid succession. Abe was at his side in a moment.

"What is it?" asked Abe, as Will fired two more shots.

"Shoot, shoot!" said Will, pointing ahead.

Abe looked in the direction indicated and saw a bull elk staggering about, fatally wounded. Abe fired a shot in its shoulder and another in the neck, when it dropped.

"I thought you had located bear when you began to shoot," said Abe, half disappointed, as they ran up through the brush and fallen timber to the elk.

"It's singular we should stumble on an elk here. Hasn't he got beautiful slim horns? I never saw such a set before."

The antlers were remarkably slim and long, with three prongs.

"Well, we can say we killed this one together," said Will, as he prepared to remove the entrails. The elk was considerably shot to pieces by six bullets, and this was a disagreeable job, but was over in fifteen minutes. Owing to the elk's weight, it was with no little difficulty that the carcass was rolled over a log and propped up in an upright position. The search up the bottom for the bears was then resumed, but seeing no trace of them, we returned to the lick by noon and thence to camp. Abe went for the horses while Will gathered up the things in camp. On our return to the main camp, Spencer said it was too late to go back for the meat and scalp that day, so on the following day Abe accompanied him. He took the two bear dogs, thinking that if the bears had remained in the vicinity he might find them. But when they returned in the afternoon, Abe reported no bear, but a very interesting time fording the river on horseback, carrying the two dogs with one hand and holding the reins and guiding the horse with the other.

Chapter VIII

Snowed In

After we had been in camp nearly a week, a swelling in Colgate's hands was observed, while that on his feet and legs had increased. These swellings caused considerable alarm, and Will, taking Colgate aside, questioned him very closely about the new trouble. Colgate insisted that he would be all right in a little while, but Will, knowing that he was accustomed to hardship and exposure, rightly attributed the cause of his ailment to something more than fatigue. After being questioned further, Colgate at last revealed the true cause of his disability, admitting that he was suffering from a trouble with which he had been afflicted for a number of years, that he had been compelled to use instruments for a long time in performing the functions of nature, which he had failed to bring with him. Will, much surprised, then asked him why he had not brought the instruments, to which he replied that he did not like to use them and thought he could do without them. From the nature of the complaint, it was evident that Colgate must have known that he did not have his instruments the very first day out from Kendrick. Yet he had persistently journeyed for eight successive days, deeper and deeper into the woods, without acquainting anyone with the fact, and knowing at the same time that the instruments were indispensable to him. Will was dumfounded. When the facts were made known to the others, all realized the serious predicament in which they were placed. What was to be done? It did not seem advisable to start him back in the rain, which was probably snow in the mountains, so it was decided to make him as comfortable as possible in camp and await fair weather. Exercise had, apparently, a bad effect on him, and we persuaded him to relinquish his duties and remain quiet, as we wished him to start out as strong as possible on the return trip. About this time, October 2nd, Spencer expressed fears that we might be snowed in, but no one deemed the danger from that source sufficiently serious to devote a day in climbing to the top of the burnt ridge to investigate the matter. The rain still continued. Colgate grew worse daily. By October 6th his legs had swollen to nearly twice their natural size, and he was barely able to move about camp without assistance. Spencer began to urge our return, and John, who did not care to hunt in the rain, vigorously seconded the motion. Abe insisted that Indian summer and milder weather must yet come before winter would set in, and that the return in the rain and snow would be undertaken under the very worst conditions for Colgate.

It was the intention to send Colgate back with the guide as soon as the weather became favorable, but when Spencer and John urged the return of the whole party so persistently, Will and Abe, who had not yet had enough hunting to satisfy them, suggested that Spencer and John return at once with Colgate, and that they would follow later, after they would have several days' more shooting. This arrangement did not, however, meet with approval. Colgate himself preferred to remain until more trophies were secured and all could return together, especially as the prospect of traveling in a snowstorm was not encouraging. This state of affairs lasted only a day or two. Finding we could wait no longer for clear weather, and Colgate's condition becoming daily more and more serious, it was finally decided to leave for Kendrick the following day, October 9th, rain or shine. It snowed all that day, and the morning was well advanced before the horses were found and brought in. The return trip was therefore postponed until the next day, when we would endeavor to make an early start.

On the morning of October 10th all arose early and breakfasted before daylight, but it was ten o'clock before all the horses were packed and the train ready to start. The snow was six inches deep at our camp. Bidding Old Jerry and Ben good-bye, we started across the flat toward the foot of the ridge. With Spencer in the lead and Colgate riding the surest-footed animal we had, we laboriously made our way up the steep ascent in the soft snow and mud. Gradually, as we neared the top of the first ridge, the snow got deeper and deeper. As we turned the brow of the ridge and followed the side of the first roundtop, the snow was about sixteen inches deep. Following the crest of the ridge, still ascending toward the Lolo Trail, the snow deepened rapidly. We pushed on until the depth of the snow got to be three feet and the horses could make their way through it only with the greatest difficulty. It was about noon and, calling a halt, the situation was discussed in detail while we ate our lunch. Spencer said, "The snow on the Lolo Trail will be at least four feet deep at the post offices. The horses can't last more than two or three days without food, and when they play out we will have to leave our stuff and walk, carrying enough grub on our backs to see us out."

What would become of Colgate? He could not walk, and in the soft snow, even if we could make crude snowshoes, it would be impossible to carry him. The trail led along steep hillsides, often overgrown for great distances with thick brush and obstructed with thousands of boulders and fallen trees. If we should attempt to pull or drag him after us under these conditions, even if there should be a crust on the snow, our progress would be necessarily so slow that several weeks would be consumed in the journey. The remaining provisions would last eight days. To continue on that route, with so meagre a supply of food and the game uncertain, involved almost certain starvation for the entire party or the eventual abandonment of Colgate to save our own lives. While the able-bodied members of the party felt confident they could make their way to Musselshell Creek (a point of safety) on crude snowshoes, they thought it would not be right to abandon Colgate until every possible means had been tired to save him. Then we thought of the river, but no one knew much about it. Spencer told us that, with the exception of two engineering corps which had passed up the river in the summer years ago, he knew of no one who had ever traveled along the river route, and expressed doubt that we would be able to take canoes or rafts safely down the river. He said, too, that there was a bad canyon somewhere below, through which it was said to be dangerous to navigate small craft and impossible to pass on horseback or on foot. He gave as his opinion that the safest and best route would be to return by trail.

As the return by trail involved the almost certain abandonment of Colgate in the snow, should he survive the cold and exposure, it became a question whether we should attempt to return by the Lolo Trail, relying for subsistence on the meagre chances of securing game, and hope, by good fortune, to succeed eventually in getting out, or to assume greater risks for our own lives and adopt the river route, which offered perhaps the most favorable prospect of getting Colgate out of the mountains.

While Spencer went ahead a quarter of a mile to make a further examination of the trail, John went to the rear to Colgate, and Will and Abe held a separate consultation. It would take several weeks to build the rafts and make our way down the river. Our relatives and friends would be subjected to the greatest anxiety and fears for our safety if we did not return at the appointed time. We knew search and relief parties would be sent out at great expense, and that in hazarding a trip down an unknown river we were taking desperate chances with our lives; but on the river there was little or no snow, and since it offered the most feasible means of getting Colgate out, we considered it our duty to forego all other considerations and attempt a passage down the river. This alternative was, of course, only possible provided arrangements could be made with one of the two men in the cabin near our recent camp for some of their provisions. When Spencer returned, the possibility of making such an arrangement was discussed, and he, knowing the prospector quite well, assured us that if the other man—Keeley—would not sell his provisions, he thought "Old Jerry" would.

As the leader of the party, Will then gave the order to turn back. By some strange premonition or instinct, the horses positively refused to turn around, and when compelled to do so, frequently left the trail and attempted to get by us and continue the other way. We, however, succeeded in getting them started back after fifteen minutes of hard work in the snow.

We arrived at our camp about four o'clock in the afternoon. A little snow had fallen in the meantime, but this was soon cleared away and the tents pitched on the same ground they had previously occupied. As soon as the horses were unsaddled, they were turned loose and allowed to roam again over the flat and the ridge above it. The day's journey had a bad effect on poor Colgate, who was almost exhausted on our arrival. That same night Will arranged with Ben Keeley, the trapper, for the sum of two hundred fifty dollars, to sell us his share of the grub in the cabin, help build our rafts, and accompany us down the river. Keeley was an excellent chopper and had considerable experience in rafting sawlogs in Minnesota and Wisconsin waters. He was, in consequence, a very valuable acquisition to our party in the emergency.

Jerry Johnson's Cabin

Our proposed trip down the river involved a number of changes in our plans and necessitated the leaving of our horses, saddles, and such other articles of our camp equipage that could be of no further service to us.

Old Jerry's cabin was not quite completed, and as we wished to leave our superfluous things with him during the winter, we thought it would be best to help him finish it, or at least get it under roof before we left. Fresh meat was needed in order to prosecute with vigor the work on the cabin, as well as on the rafts later. Ben and Spencer, being the best choppers, were accordingly delegated to assist Jerry with the cabin, while Will, Abe, and John hunted.

The deep snows on the mountains and the recent stormy weather had driven the elk and deer down into the valleys and river bottoms. The day after our return it cleared off, and the bright sunlight, the first we had seen since the 26th of September, was most acceptable and cheering.

The snow disappeared on the banks of the river, life in camp became cheerful and pleasant, and game being abundant, an ample supply of fresh meat was readily secured. In four days the roof of Jerry's cabin was finished, and with the exception of one day, during which it rained, the weather was exceptionally fine.

Chapter IX

A Hunt at the Lower Warm Springs

The program for the following morning was a hunt at the lower lick. On retiring that night, in order to get as early a start as possible, it was agreed that the first one who awakened in the morning should call the others.

"Abe! Hello, Abe! What time is it?" asked Will—Abe and John having the only running watches in the camp at that time.

In a minute there was a flash of light as Abe struck a match.

"Pshaw, it's only quarter-past twelve!" said Abe disgustedly as he rolled over in his blankets.

Two hours later Abe awoke and struck another match. It was still too early. Will was the first to wake after that, and it was then daylight. He jumped up quickly, calling Abe and John. It was still raining, the dull pounding of the drops on the tent being anything but encouraging for a prospective hunt. John said he was not feeling well and did not wish to go that morning. So Abe and Will, after hastily eating a sandwich, started off at a brisk pace down the trail.

"Will this rain ever stop?" asked Abe impatiently, as he thrust aside the dripping branches of a young fir tree which projected into the trail, thereby causing a miniature shower under it.

"It must be the rainy season," said Will.

"Well, I'm sick of it. I never hunted so hard before in all my life in such weather, but as we can't stay much longer and I want to kill elk, it's a 'groundhog case.'"

Several small brooks were crossed at intervals. When within a quarter of a mile of the lick, a peculiar sound— half whistle, half bellow—was faintly heard.

Will stopped short and said, "Listen!"

The same sound was repeated.

"Elk!" said Will positively.

"Are you sure?" asked Abe.

"Certain; the same sound that mine made the other day."

"Jove! We're in luck at last!" replied Abe.

As the lick was approached, we became more and more cautious. Abe was in the lead and did not move faster than ten feet a minute.

When in sight of the lick, he stopped and remained motionless a full minute. Then he turned and whispered, "There's something in."

Will was moving up closer when Abe raised his hand to motion him back, whispering, "Stand still!"

Just then a cow elk (for that was what he had seen when he first noted a movement through the brush and timber) walked out into the open lick in full view, looking squarely at Abe. It is, of course, well known that when game does not scent the hunter, even if he is in plain view, the game does not become alarmed as long as the hunter remains motionless.

Abe was just stepping over a protruding limb as the elk appeared, with one leg poised in the air and one hand extended toward Will. He was obliged to remain in that uncomfortable position for a full half-minute before the elk's suspicions were satisfied and she lowered her head to lick. Both of us then took positions behind trees near us and waited. In a moment a second cow and a calf entered the lick, followed by a third cow. After the lapse of a minute the bull appeared over the brow of the hill, entered the lick and, passing along the edge of it, entered the woods, standing in such a position that his head and the forward part of his body were concealed behind some trees. He remained in this position for some time, while the balance of the herd were patronizing the lick. We were getting impatient.

"Shoot!" said Will, as the calf came out of the lick and walked to the side of the bull. "They are moving off now."

Just then the bull stepped forward far enough to enable Abe to see his shoulder.

Bang! went his gun, and a second later, bang! bang! went Will's double-barrel.

In a single bound the bull was out of sight over the brow of the hill with Abe in swift pursuit.

At the report of the guns, the balance of the herd became alarmed and started to run across a cedar flat adjacent to the lick and about a hundred feet above the river bottom.

Will had selected a young cow, as the camp was in need of meat, and gave her two shots as she was making off. He failed to stop her, however, and also started in pursuit.

The tracks of the bull were easy to follow, as he took terrific leaps down the hill, ploughing great furrows in the ground at every jump. On reaching the bottom, however, he turned sharply to the right and followed a game trail at the base of the hill. By his tracks, Abe soon saw that his pace was slackening, and from the blood which could be seen along the trail it was evident the bull was badly wounded.

Going along cautiously, Abe finally saw the bull standing perfectly still in the trail, about seventy-five yards ahead of him. Taking careful aim, he pulled the trigger, but his gun snapped. Working the lever which operated the magazine, without taking his eye off the elk, the gun snapped again. A hasty examination showed that the gun was disabled so that it was returning the empty shell into the barrel instead of ejecting it. Hastily inserting a new cartridge in the barrel, Abe was nearly ready to shoot when bang! bang! went Will's double-barrel in the flat above, and with two bounds the bull was out of sight.

We will not attempt to reproduce what Abe said just then, but he followed the tracks to a small ravine, where they turned abruptly down to the river. Halting for a moment here, Abe examined the shore of the river ahead and spied the bull standing in the river near the shore, facing the opposite side of the river. Blood could be seen oozing from a wound through the lungs, back of the shoulder and just above the heart.

Abe had reached a little rocky point about forty feet above the river and about seventy yards from where the elk was standing. Here was an interesting problem. If Abe shot the elk again while it was facing the opposite shore, even if he broke its shoulders, the elk might have sufficient vitality to struggle into the deep water and be washed down the river. With his left elbow resting on his knee, Abe covered the elk with his gun and waited. In a few minutes the bull lay down in the river, nothing but his head showing above the surface of the water.

Suddenly the report of Will's gun rang out again, and with a start the bull sprang up and took several jumps toward the opposite shore, but soon stopped, facing downstream. A moment later he faced the near shore and Abe, thinking a shot through the heart might cause him to spring out of the river to the shore, fired again.

On the contrary, however, the bull turned and made for the opposite shore. When nearly across, he began to stagger and wave his beautiful antlers from side to side. Fearing he would expire in the river and be washed down, Abe fired a shot into the rear portion of his body, hoping the effect might be to cause the bull to make for the opposite shore, but the scheme did not succeed.

Standing in the swift, roaring stream up to his knees, savagely trampling the rocky bottom of the river in his endeavor to maintain equilibrium, he gracefully poised his magnificent head in the air, while above him, mute witnesses of his sad distress, towered his native mountains. The dying elk and the surroundings formed a picture such as brush and pigment can never hope to reproduce.

At last the rear portion of his body fell over sidewise, carrying the front part with it. With a violent effort, the elk stood erect, only to fall again. Lying in the water, he continued to fight the encroachments of death, the swift current and his struggles carrying him downstream, but his struggles became more and more feeble and finally ceased altogether when the carcass lodged against a rock in the river.

"Hello, old 'stuff!' I hear you've killed the prize bull elk," said Will delightedly as he appeared over the edge of the bank above, having heard Abe's last shot and seen the elk lodged against the rock near the other shore.

"Hurry up! Let's get him out before he washes down the river," continued Will.

"Hold on, Will! Don't you wade out into that cold water," said Abe, but Will had already removed his trousers and started in. He soon got over to the elk and then motioned Abe not to follow.

He made the elk secure by piling some stones back of it and bending the neck so that the horns acted as a prop. Will then forded to the opposite side to exercise his legs and restore the circulation of the blood, as the cold water had numbed them. Selecting a pole with which to steady himself, he recrossed the river.

"Did you get yours too?" asked Abe, referring to the elk Will was after.

"You bet!" said Will. "We'll go right over to it."

In a few minutes Will was ready, and both walked back to the lick.

They found the elk lying head downward on a steep hillside. She was young and very fat, so good meat was assured. The elk, after being shot by Will at the lick, had gone around in a semicircular course, and after receiving five shots while running, had fallen dead within twenty yards of the lick.

When Will and Abe returned to camp, they found Spencer, Ben Keeley, and Jerry Johnson just on the eve of starting down the river with five packhorses to bring in a lot of shakes that Keeley had made to roof the cabin. Consequently, no time was lost in getting up the horses to pack in the meat, horns, and scalp.

The shakes were on the trail to the lick about a mile and a half distant from camp. Will, being wet and somewhat chilled, donned dry clothes, while Abe accompanied the train down the trail. When the shakes were reached, Spencer assisted Jerry to pack the animals, while Keeley and Abe passed on to the lick, riding two of the horses.

Two young cow elk and a calf were surprised in the lick, one of which Abe shot, mistaking it, on account of its size, for a deer. Keeley immediately bled it and had just finished removing the entrails when Spencer arrived on the scene. The three then continued down the river to where Abe's bull was, and descending the steep bank, tied up the horses and set about to devise some plan to get the elk ashore.

After discussing the situation in detail, Spencer said the best plan would be to ford the river to the elk on horseback, cut off the head and drag it across the river by a rope fastened to the pommel of Keeley's saddle.

The plan seemed feasible, and Keeley and Spencer started into the river, while Abe soon had a warm fire going on shore. All went very well until Spencer got near the carcass of the elk and the horse he was riding snorted and refused to proceed farther. The horse was finally prevailed upon to approach near enough to allow Spencer to jump off onto the carcass of the elk. Keeley then took both horses to the opposite shore and held them while Spencer cut off the elk's head with a hatchet.

When this was done, Keeley brought back the horses to Spencer, who gave him a rope, one end of which was tied to the elk's horns. Keeley fastened the other end to his saddle and started across the river, dragging the head through the swift water. In a short time he reached the shore, followed by Spencer.

The head was then carried to the fire, and while Spencer removed the scalp and cleaned the skull, Abe and Keeley repaired to the lick and secured the choice portions of the two cow elk.

When Spencer came up, the horses were packed, and the meat, horns, and scalp taken into camp.

Chapter X

Building the Rafts

On the morning of October 15th, five days after our unsuccessful attempt to reach the Lolo Trail, Spencer and Keeley went down the river to look for suitable timber for the rafts. Will was laid up in camp with a bad boil on the ankle of his right foot, and Abe had a sore neck from a wrench he had received while out hunting a few days before. Colgate grew gradually worse. The weather at this time remained clear and warm. The snow was rapidly disappearing on the hillsides adjacent to the river, and notwithstanding the temporary ailments from which some of us were suffering, we were all cheerful and hopeful.

In the afternoon Abe went down the river to see what success Spencer and Keeley had met with in their search for timber. He found them near the lower warm springs, where a bunch of dead white cedars of suitable size had been located, some of which had already been felled and peeled. Abe took a block of the wood, and after ascertaining its specific gravity by use of a small fish scale belonging to Will, he calculated the number of cubic feet each of the two rafts should contain in order to carry their respective loads. The object was to avoid unnecessary and superfluous weight, which would make the rafts more difficult to handle in the swift water.

That night quite a debate was indulged in concerning the rafts. Abe and Will insisted that a long, narrow raft was the only form that could possibly pass through the numerous projecting boulders in the river, while Keeley and Spencer were equally sure that a wider raft of less length was best. Keeley and Spencer were, however, won over, and the dimensions of the rafts were finally fixed at four and a half to five feet wide and twenty-six feet long.

Camp at Warm Springs

In order to avoid the long walk back and forth from where the rafts were being built, a camp was established near them the following day, and Keeley and Spencer moved down. With Will still unable to walk on his sore foot and remaining in bed, we were compelled for a time to maintain two camps. Colgate required considerable nursing, and fires had to be kept going for his comfort. John and Abe were consequently kept busy most of the time cooking and getting in necessary firewood. Every afternoon, however, Abe would go down to the other camp and help for several hours on the rafts, carrying such additional provisions as the other camp required along with him. About this time myriads of snow geese passed over us daily as they migrated southward.

One afternoon, as Abe was going down to the other camp, just as he was crossing a little ravine, he noted a movement through the brush in the bottom to his left. Standing still, he waited a moment and then saw the head of a deer and soon afterward the body, moving up the ravine toward the trail. As the deer disappeared back of some bushes, Abe sat down in the trail. When the deer struck the trail, it turned toward Abe; and as it approached, and less brush intervened between them, Abe saw that it was a blacktail doe, preceded by a fawn. The wind was moving from them toward Abe, so they could not scent him. On they came, nearer and nearer. The graceful antics of the fawn as it moved its head up and down and from side to side, intently watching and listening, was greatly admired and enjoyed by Abe. At last, when within fifty feet of him, both fawn and doe became suspicious and stopped. Abe sat perfectly motionless, with his gun pointed at them, and did not even blink his eyes. A gentle breeze from the opposite direction enabled them to scent him, and at the same instant the fawn made a phenomenal leap to the right of the trail, while the doe turned squarely about and darted down the trail like an arrow. Through the opening in the timber Abe could catch glimpses of the fawn as it circled about to join the doe far down the river.

The building of the rafts was no small undertaking. The river was full of boulders, and the shores were a mass of jagged rocks. The heavy rafts in the swift water could not be so completely controlled that they would not strike the boulders and ledges occasionally, and for that reason had to be built very strong and firm. Having no spikes or bolts, we had to resort to framing and dovetailing methods in their construction.

On account of its lightness, dead cedar was selected as the best timber available for the purpose. Straight trees, sixteen to twenty inches in diameter, were chosen, felled, and peeled. As the horses could not be utilized on account of the rough ground, fallen timber, and want of suitable harness, the work of collecting the logs on the riverbank was a difficult job and involved some heavy lifting. With skis, rollers, and handspikes, we moved the logs of the first raft in one day to the riverbank and placed them side by side on top of two crosslogs.

With the aid of a wooden square and a scribing awl, made by Abe, the logs were marked and the work of fastening them together begun. Our tools consisted of two axes, two hatchets, a broken crosscut saw and an inch auger, the last two belonging to Jerry Johnson and having been borrowed from him.

Dovetails were sawed in each of the logs opposite each other at both ends and in the middle. Crosspieces of green fir were dressed out to fit into the dovetails loosely, and then, with thin wedges split from cedar, the logs were wedged tightly to the crosspieces. The ends of the crosspieces were also wedged to prevent the logs from spreading apart. To still further strengthen the rafts, vertical keys, four inches square, were set in the joints between the logs, the mortises extending halfway into each log. Cedar poles, three to four inches in diameter, were then pinned down around the outside edge, forming a sort of railing. As Spencer and Keeley expected to man this raft, the lesser details of construction were left to their own choice. They made a framework capable of supporting the provisions, six to eight inches above the top of the raft in its middle portion. A large sweep was mounted in the stern, and several upright posts were framed into the raft at convenient places. On October 22nd the first raft was ready to launch and was named the "Clearwater." The same day the upper camp was abandoned. Some of the things were left in a small tent and subsequently taken over to Jerry's cabin, and the rest were packed on horses to where the rafts were being built.

The work was then prosecuted with greater vigor. Abe, Keeley and Spencer worked regularly on the rafts, while Will did the cooking and cared for Colgate. John assisted Will and occasionally went over and helped on the raft.

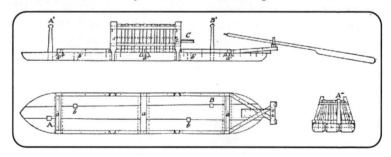

The "Carlin"

The dimensions of the second raft were the same as the first, but larger timber was used, and the logs were hewed on two sides. Instead of a framework, a sort of a box was built in the middle of the raft, with a raised floor, in which the provisions could be more conveniently carried. The second raft was completed about October 29th. No suitable name for this raft suggested itself at that time, but during the voyage down the river, the second raft, to distinguish it from the other, soon came to be known as the "Carlin."

While the rafts were being built we kept a sharp lookout on the trail. Spencer made two examinations, which necessitated the laborious climbing of the high ridge and a hard pull through the snow each time. The first of these was made on October 18th. After reaching the top of the ridge, he found the snow was thawing on the hillsides having southern exposures, but it remained intact on the north hillsides. A stiff crust had formed on the snow, and traveling for horses was very difficult. A very curious fact which Spencer noted as he journeyed on was that some of the horses had passed over the trail recently. When he reached the point where we had stopped and turned back eight days before, he was surprised to find that some of the horses had been there. By the tracks and the area they had pawed over in their search for food, he could see that they had spent two nights in the snow, after which some of them had again returned to the river bottom, while others had gone down into a deep gulch to one side of the trail. The horses evidently had made an unsuccessful attempt to get out of the woods. Spencer pressed on a half mile farther with great difficulty, and finding the snow was getting deeper, returned to camp and reported the trail in worse shape than when we had made the attempt to get out, with the snow now probably six feet deep on the Lolo Trail.

A curious incident of this trip of Spencer's was the finding of a gold watch charm, which had been lost by one of the members of the party in a mass of rocks which the trail crossed. The rocks were so located that the sun's rays fell vertically upon them and thawed the snow so as to allow the lost watch charm to be seen.

The last examination of the trail was made by Spencer on October 30th, just before starting down the river on the rafts. The snow had apparently thawed considerably since his previous examination, and all hoped that we might yet be able to take Colgate out over the Lolo Trail. On his return, however, Spencer informed us that while the snow had disappeared in the river bottoms, it had really increased in depth on the high ridges, and that it would be utterly impossible to take horses out over the trail.

We were out of fresh meat, as we had abandoned hunting and given our whole attention to the rafts after October 22nd. Will had, however, succeeded in catching a few fish nearly every day, which were very palatable in the absence of meat.

The same day that Spencer went to examine the trail the last time, Abe went hunting, leaving the camp at daylight. He was very fortunate in finding a young cow elk about four miles up the river, which he shot, bringing the heart and a piece of the sirloin with him to camp that evening. The next day he and Spencer started out with two horses and brought in the meat.

The same day, October 31st, Abe and Will went to Jerry's cabin and selected as much of Keeley's provisions as they thought sufficient for the trip down the river, leaving the remainder with Jerry. We expected to make the passage down the river in about a week, and although Jerry assured us it would not take more than four days, about fifteen days' provisions were taken as a safeguard. We had been out of sugar and milk for some time and were therefore anxious to buy some of Jerry's, as we had already used all of Keeley's sugar. Jerry, however, refused to part with any of his, saying he had little enough for himself. Abe offered him his entire fishing outfit, valued at $22, for two pounds of sugar, which Jerry refused. Will then offered him a 45-90-300 Winchester single-shot rifle (which he had bought from Keeley), a lot of ammunition, and fishing hooks and tackle, for three pounds of sugar, which was accepted. They then presented Jerry with all their horses and asked him to care for them during the winter and try and save them, if possible, from starvation. The following day Will brought the provisions down to camp.

After October 22nd, when we moved Colgate to the lower camp, he failed rapidly. Liquid had collected in his lungs, which choked or smothered him when he assumed a horizontal position, and he was thus unable to lie down. Spencer made him a chair out of a block of wood, upon which he sat day and night. His legs were swollen enormously, and although a small man when well, he then weighed fully two hundred pounds. He was perfectly helpless and had to be assisted when he wished to move the smallest distance about camp. He was very sensitive to cold, and we constantly kept blankets around him. We were, besides, compelled to divide the night into watches and sit up with him, maintaining fires all night long for his comfort. Scarcely an hour passed that he did not require assistance, but notwithstanding the most careful nursing and attention to his requirements, he grew steadily worse. On the 2nd of November the swelling on one of his legs broke. Considerable liquid was discharged, after which he felt somewhat relieved.

Knowing that we could return over the trail on snowshoes if disencumbered by Colgate, someone suggested that Jerry Johnson should take care of Colgate until we could return to Kendrick, when a relief party could be sent after Colgate, with additional supplies for Johnson. Old Jerry refused to agree to this, however, on account of the uncertainty of a relief party being able to reach him at that season, and asserted that the remaining provisions were barely sufficient for himself during the winter. Colgate was, besides, afraid of Johnson and was unwilling to stay with him.

Colgate's rapidly sinking condition argued strongly against such a course. It was doubtful if he could survive the journey out, and it was almost certain that he could not live until rescued by a relief party, even if such a party were to start back for him immediately after our return to civilization. The only humane course left us, therefore, was to attempt a passage down the river and restore Colgate to his family before his dissolution, if possible.

On the morning of November 2nd, the river was running full of broken ice, but it passed off during the day. Will walked down the river several miles to examine the rapids. On his return he reported two large ones, one of which he considered quite dangerous, and said that the only open channel through it was on the left-hand side. The final arrangements for the trip down the river kept everybody in camp busy. The rafts were launched and a number of poles prepared for guiding them. Abe filed the saw for Old Jerry. John sewed up two sacks of flour in waterproof canvas to prevent them from getting wet. Will made himself a shirt and mittens out of a blanket, the weather being very cold. John also made himself a similar pair of mittens and a hood, but subsequently gave the latter to Colgate. Everything being ready on the night of November 2nd, we decided to start the following morning as early as possible.

The journey down the river was undertaken with a full sense of its probable hardships and dangers. We feared it, because we reasoned that were it a practicable and easy route, many hunters and prospectors would have preferred to travel up and down the river in canoes rather than go around by way of the Lolo Trail with a more expensive outfit. Since no one, except engineering corpsmen in 1881 and 1886 had ever been known to pass through the canyon (which was said to be somewhere below on the river), and then in the summer when the water was low, we feared we would find dangerous and perhaps impassable places in the river at this season. So serious an undertaking did Will and Abe consider it that they wrote a number of letters, which they left with Jerry Johnson to mail when he would return to Missoula the following summer.

Chapter XI

Down the Kooskooskee

Throughout the trip, at each day's end, Will Carlin recorded daily events in his diary. What follows here in Chapters XI and XII was taken almost verbatim from that diary.

Friday, November 3rd, 1893 — We were through breakfast shortly after daylight, packed up everything in the most convenient form and loaded the rafts. Although we hurried as much as possible, it was eleven o'clock before we were ready to start down the river. Old Jerry came down early in the morning to see us off and take some letters which we wished to leave with him to post to our families in the spring in case we never got out of the mountains. This morning it was cold and cloudy; it began to rain hard about the time we started. It was half-past eleven when Keeley and Spencer, who manned the lighter raft, shoved off from shore and started down the river. Our raft followed at a distance of about one hundred yards. We had easy water for the first half-mile, when we landed our raft, and John went down around the point to see if Keeley and Spencer got through the first bad rapid all right. He returned in fifteen minutes and reported that the boys had passed through safely and had landed on the opposite bank below the rapid. We shoved off and stuck on a small rock, but got off in a few minutes. Jerry gave us a parting salute of three shots, and we waved him good-bye. When we rounded the point, Spencer motioned us toward his side of the river. We entered the rapid and just got through the narrow channel without touching the big rocks on either side. Our raft was heavier than theirs and more difficult to land, so we kept right on past them, and rounding the point two hundred yards below, we entered the second bad rapid, of which I had spoken the day before.

This was a difficult place to get through, as the current carried us toward the right bank at the head of the rapid and the only open channel was along the left-hand side. We had gotten about one-third through when we struck two large rocks with great force. Not being able to keep the stern from swinging, in a moment we were sidewise to the current, jammed against the rocks. The water rushed over the raft and turned its bottom against the rocks, with its side down, and over half the raft was under water. John was thrown off the bow, but he kept hold of his pike pole and managed to get in shallow water and thence to the shore. Colgate was sucked under the raft and was on the point of being swept away when Abe caught him by the collar of his coat and pulled him onto the upper side of the raft. Little Montana was drowning, but she was also pulled out high and dry.

Spencer and Keeley saw our upset from above the rapid in time to run their raft ashore. They came down and tried to wade out to us, but could get only a few feet from shore without being washed off their feet. It was impossible to make them understand a word, owing to the roaring of the water, although we were only about twenty yards apart. Finally we managed to make them understand that we wanted them to tie their rope to a tree about one hundred feet above us and let their raft down so that they could get over to us and take off our load. It took over an hour to accomplish this. Spencer attended to the rope, and Keeley guided his raft through the rocks along the shore.

We sent Colgate, the dogs, and some provisions over in the first load. Abe helped Keeley to land, while I stayed on the raft and got out a second load of blankets, etc. John had worked up the riverbank and found a shallow place, where he managed with great difficulty to cross to our side of the river. Colgate and he were cold from the icy water and sleet, which was falling heavily, so Spencer built them a fire. We had just transferred our second load when our raft, relieved of its weight, rose in the water and partially righted. Abe jumped on, and we loosened it from the rocks and started down the river. We got through the rapid without any further mishap, but could not make a landing below. My pike pole was jammed in the rocks in the river bottom and jerked out of my hands. We were carried down for half a mile, when we managed to run fast on a bunch of small rocks in shallow water near the shore, which prevented us from being carried into the rapid below. Wading ashore, we made the raft fast to a root with a rope and struck out for camp. We all made as comfortable a camp as possible, hustled in firewood for the night, and cooked supper. It continued raining and sleeting. All in all, we'd had a rough sort of a day. The night was divided into watches so that a fire could be kept up for Colgate.

Saturday, November 4th — We decided to leave our antlers and all other unnecessary things with Jerry and lighten our loads as much as possible. Spencer walked up to get him to come down with horses and pack the things to his cabin. Keeley, Abe, and I went down to get the raft off the rocks. John remained in camp to take care of Colgate. After two hours' hard work in the water, we got the raft off and pulled it ashore. Returning to camp, we built a rousing big fire and soon dried all our stuff. Spencer returned at three o'clock and said that Jerry would be down in the morning. We got in firewood for the night. It rained hard nearly all day. Colgate was not as well today as yesterday, due, I am afraid, to the wetting he got.

Sunday, November 5th — We got up at daylight and packed up all the things we intended taking with us. Placing them on Spencer's raft, we carefully let it down the rapid to where the other lay and transferred one-half the load to our raft. Jerry came down about ten o'clock to get the things we intended leaving with him. Having helped him pack the horses, we said good-bye to him again and started down the river at eleven o'clock, with Keeley and Spencer in the lead.

Several pretty bad rapids were passed, and the first island was sighted about half-past eleven. Finding the right-hand channel too shallow, we were obliged to take the left-hand, which has some rather bad rocks at the end of the island. Spencer and Keeley stuck, but got off without much difficulty. By keeping more to the left, we got through without trouble, and all made a landing below the island on the right bank.

Abe went down the river to examine the rapids below. This island was merely a gravel bar with a few pine trees on it. I had no doubt that in summer the right-hand channel would be practically dry. A large creek entered the river just below the island. It drained a fine flat that I had examined some days before and found full of elk and bear signs. Abe returned, and having found a landing place below, we started again at about half-past one and made a good run until we came to a rapid worse than any we had yet seen. Spencer and Keeley tried to keep along the right-hand bank and stuck fast on a rock. They motioned us to keep to the center. This brought us into the worst of the water, with large boulders on every side. We were going along at a tremendous rate when two large rocks loomed up on each side of us, the water falling vertically several feet below them. Thinking it out of the question to pass them, and fully expecting an upset, I shouted to Colgate to hold fast to the posts. We were so fortunate, however, as to get exactly between them, and our raft shot over the drop into the quieter water below. Keeley afterward remarked, "I thought you fellows were goners that time, sure! We couldn't see anything of you after you took the jump." Making a landing below, we went up to help Spencer and Keeley, but they had jumped into the water above their waists and lifted the raft off the rock and were leading it down along the shore.

Making another examination of the river, we found several stiff rapids—one in particular, where the river narrowed down and went through a gorge. The waves were over four feet high, but the rocks were all hidden by high water. Our raft went ahead, and we had no trouble until we came to the gorge. Here we rolled around like an ocean steamer and came very near upsetting. It's lucky the rocks were covered. The waves struck Abe, who stood in the bow, above the waist and came near carrying him off the raft. A landing was made to wait for the other raft, which, however, passed us and took the lead. We found no more bad places, and after going perhaps three-quarters of a mile, we saw that Spencer and Keeley had landed and were motioning us toward them. Although we worked as hard as we could, we could not quite reach the bank and came near getting caught on some large rocks at the mouth of a creek which came in from the right. As we passed the other raft, we threw out a rope, which fell short. Spencer, however, caught a second rope and was dragged off his feet into the water. He held on and snubbed the raft, so that we managed to land about twenty yards below them. It being about half-past three, we decided to camp. It has rained hard all day, and everyone is wet. Our camp is on a damp flat with very little dry wood. Some put up the tent and fly, others cut and carried in wood until after dark. After supper, we laid a raised floor of dry cedar under the fly to put our provisions on and made a big fire to dry our blankets. We did not get to bed until after two a.m. The dogs have been excitedly sniffing the air and, from the signs we have seen, elk must frequent the flat.

Monday, November 6th — We got up at daylight, and after breakfast Abe and I walked down the river three miles. The walking was harder than the rafting. On the way down we saw old camps and choppings of surveyors. It had rained hard all night, and the river was very high. We saw two very bad rapids, besides many minor ones. Got back to camp at twelve o'clock and found that Spencer and Keeley had made a bow oar, as the water was getting too deep in places to use poles advantageously. We started down the river with Spencer and Keeley in the lead. We all had exceptionally good luck in missing big boulders a dozen times or more. Spencer made a landing on the second island and helped us land by the aid of a rope. The left-hand channel was found to be too dangerous to run, as the current flows directly against a ledge of sharp rocks which we could not pass. The right-hand channel was still more dangerous, for the current swept against a large rock in the center of the river. On the right side of it there were some six large boulders reaching to the shore. To get by this point safely it would have been necessary to run the rafts between the big rock and the island, which was obviously impossible in the swift current. We therefore landed on the island and let the rafts, by ropes, down past the big rock to the foot of the island. This prevented us from examining the river beyond. We could see the waves of a very long and hard rapid below us. There was, however, no alternative but to run ahead and take the chances of finding a fall below.

Spencer and Keeley went ahead. We climbed a big pile of driftwood, which the water in freshet time had piled up twenty feet high, and watched them. We saw them enter the rapid, then make a swift shoot out of sight to the right. Their disappearance was so sudden that it almost took our breath away. After a minute's anxious watching, we saw them below the rapid, mere specks in the distance, and found out afterward that they had several close shaves. We entered the rapid in the center. The waves were the highest we had yet seen, and we would have been upset if we had not been careful in balancing the raft. These rapids were two hundred yards long, and although the roughest water we had experienced so far, there were no rocks in sight. The riverbanks were perpendicular at this point, and we could not have landed if we had wished to.

Below the rapid was a very deep pool over half a mile long. We found Spencer and Keeley landed on a nice, dry island covered with trees, and as it was half-past three, camp was made. On the island we found the only fresh signs of man (Indians) we had yet seen. There was a trail crossing the river at this point. Evidently the Indians camp here in summer when crossing from the Lolo to the trail on the divide to the south.

We had been out four days now and had not made much more than ten miles. Keeley was anxious to turn the rafts loose and trust to luck in running through, but the others did not consider it safe at all, as we didn't know what was below us. It continued to rain hard, and we were pretty well tired out. Our things were all so wet that we decided to remain here the next day. Some of us would dry the blankets, clothes, and provisions, and the rest would go down the river some distance to examine the rapids. A comfortable camp was made and a rousing big fire built. I tried fishing, but had no success owing to high water. This island is one hundred yards long by twenty-five wide. We found some old tepee poles and a sweatbath. The right-hand channel would be easy to ford in low water.

Tuesday, November 7th — It was clear this morning, and we were up and through breakfast soon after daylight. Abe decided to go down the river and examine the rapids. The rest of us busied ourselves around camp—some dried blankets, others provisions. Spencer made a bow oar for us. Abe did not get in until dark, very tired and hungry, having had no food but a small piece of bread since morning. He had walked eight miles down the river and reported the first five miles fair going, but the last three a continuous rapid of very swift water, owing to the exceptional fall of the riverbed. He thinks we cannot run these rapids at all and will have to let the rafts down by ropes all the way.

Wednesday, November 8th — We made an exceptionally early start this morning and made five miles in a very short time with three stops. The runs were exciting but not dangerous. On the way down Abe called my attention to a pile of rocks on a high bluff, which he had observed the preceding day and named "Monk's Point" owing to their wonderful likeness to the figure of a hooded monk seated on a rock, with his head bent down as in thought. We landed at two large eddies from which we could see the river below take a sudden shoot down like a millrace. We passed a beautiful creek, which emptied into the river from the left in a succession of miniature falls. John went with Keeley and Spencer today.

Four of us went down to examine Abe's bad rapids, and John stayed with the rafts. We found by far the worst rapids we had yet seen. The current was extremely swift for a mile, and the river full of boulders. Then the river narrowed, and in the center was a very large rock which left narrow channels on each side, and these were full of rocks. Below, it was still worse—more boulders and worse water. It was clear that we would upset a good many times before getting through this rapid if we were to try to run it, and should we fail to make a landing, we would be carried into a row of rocks that would smash us up completely. We cannot lower the rafts by ropes from the right-hand shore owing to perpendicular banks in many places. It would be unsafe to leave Colgate on the raft while passing through the worst places, and the right-hand bank was so steep and rough that he could not be helped along it at all. We returned toward evening and made camp. Tried fishing, but got only one strike. Some of us think we are at the canyon, but Spencer thinks not.

A Cold Morning

Thursday, November 9th — We awoke to find it drizzling and cold this morning. Got ready as soon as possible and started to cross the river. About two hundred yards below the camp there was a fall in the river, and to be sure that we would not be caught in the current (from which escape would be impossible, and which would carry us over the falls), we pulled our rafts upstream to the head of the eddies and started across from there. Spencer and Keeley took the lead and made the gravel bar just at the head of the rapid. The left-hand channel was all right, and after running aground on some small rocks, they made the opposite shore and landed. We in turn made the bar, but owing to bad poling our raft turned sidewise in the channel.

I jumped out into shallow water and with a rope tried to hold the stern upstream, but was promptly swept off my feet and was wet to the neck before I could regain them. We landed some yards below the other raft.

Here we all got off, except Colgate, who could not walk along the rocky shore, and Keeley who was to guide the raft with a pole around the rocks. The rest of us let it down the shore with a long rope. Things went smoothly enough until we got to the large rock in the center of the stream. The water was so terrific that we thought it best to take Colgate off the raft while passing this place. We helped Colgate up to a small flat just back of the river, and John stayed to assist him. Then two of us took the end of the rope down the river, and one stood just above the rock to snub the raft when it entered the narrow channel. The raft was allowed to run downstream about thirty yards through the worst water. We then tried to snub it, but its momentum was too much for us, and we were all dragged along through the water and over the rocks for some yards. The next mile was very hard work. We had little space to work in and were pulled off our feet and dragged a good many times. When about fifty yards from the small eddy we had picked out as our camping place, we attempted to run the raft between some large rocks. It moved so fast, however, that we could not stop it, and it ran aground on a large gravel bar or point. It was raining hard, and Colgate was so cold that we thought it best to build a fire for him immediately.

Keeley would not let his raft down with the rope, but insisted on running the rapids. We didn't think it the best plan, but as it was his raft we said no more about it. Keeley, Spencer, and Abe went back. The last named was to stand at a point where the current made into the shore and throw them a rope in case they failed to land, then they would lead down from there and thus escape the worst water. John and I unloaded our raft, got in wood for the night, and tried to get a fire going for Colgate. Everything was soaked, and it took us over an hour to get the fire started. Colgate was so stiff that he could not move.

Just before dark Abe came to camp and told us that Keeley had failed to land, that their raft had upset on a large rock, and that they were in a bad position; and as nearly all our provisions were on their raft, we had to try to get it off that night. We gathered all the ropes we could find and hurried to where they were. The raft was sidewise on the rocks, and about half of it was held under the water by the current. Spencer had a narrow escape from drowning, being nearly washed away when the raft went under. Although we worked hard, we could not budge the raft, so we put a rope to the bow and another to the stern and fastened them to trees. I built a fire with a piece of dry cedar, while Abe helped Spencer and Keeley get ashore on the rope. It was then quite dark, and we had a rough time walking back to camp. After supper a large fire was built. Spencer had a great knack of making a good fire out of almost anything. We put up our tent and dried our few blankets as best we could. Half our bedding is on the other raft. We've had a very hard day, and everyone is completely tired out. It is not raining now, but is growing very cold.

Friday, November 10th — Although fairly tired out last night, we found it difficult to sleep because of the cold. There being insufficient covering and our clothes thoroughly drenched, it was not surprising that we were up and through a hasty breakfast soon after daylight. Upon looking at our raft, just above camp, we found quite a lot of ice on it. The air was cold and clear. Immediately after breakfast we went up to the other raft and found it as firmly lodged as it had been the night before. The water seemed to have fallen slightly. We hastily constructed a small raft of three logs held together by ropes. Keeley went on this to the raft in the river. The small raft was pulled back, and Spencer went over in the same manner. The canvas covering of the load was loosened, and the provisions were loaded on the small raft and safely landed; the rest of the cargo in like manner. The load being off, we found it possible to dislodge the raft from the rocks, and we pulled it into shore a few yards below. Keeley and Spencer were stiff with cold, so we built a fire and warmed up before proceeding farther.

We decided that it was safer to carry the provisions overland on our backs than to trust them to the raft. Some of us did this while the others let the raft down by ropes, arriving at camp at half past three, tired and hungry. After dinner, having a little daylight left, some got in the night's firewood while the others made a hasty examination of the river below us for a quarter of a mile. Upon their return they reported the water tremendously swift and that the rocks were more numerous and dangerous than any we had yet seen. In fact, they saw one place ahead that looked impassable, but did not have time to get down near it. This was very disagreeable news, for our ropes were becoming frayed and weak from constant contact with sharp rocks and would not endure much more work of this kind. If they should break while we were letting a raft through a bad place, it would mean the probable death of those on board and the certain loss of the provisions. We were also worried about Colgate, who seemed to be failing very rapidly in strength and in mind. He hardly said a word all day except when he was spoken to, or at mealtime when he was given his food. He sat and gazed for hours with a vacant stare at the river or the rocks. His legs look very bad indeed and are evidently mortified from the knees down. We found today that our flour is getting very low; only about forty pounds are left. We've decided to eat no more of it at present, but to live on cornmeal and beans as long as they last. We are out of fresh meat. I tried to catch some fish, but they would not rise. We hope this might be the much talked of canyon and that we will soon be through it.

Saturday, November 11th — It is still cold and clear. We went down the river a long way this morning and were horrified to find that we are absolutely stuck. Half a mile below camp is a ledge of rocks and a rapid through which we cannot take a raft. Below this are two more places still worse. Everyone gave his opinion of his own accord that we cannot get our rafts farther down the river.

Our position is as follows: We have barely one week's short allowance of flour left. All our other provisions, except a few pounds of cornmeal and beans and a handful of salt each, are exhausted. The shores of the river are a mass of irregular rocks. Numerous ledges or cliffs, some of them hundreds of feet high, rise vertically above the river and project into it. The hillsides adjacent are steep and rocky and covered with dense brush. Many of the ledges are so precipitous that it is all an able-bodied man can do to hang to bushes and climb around them on narrow clefts or steps in the rock. Most of us are considerably weakened from exposure and are not in a fit condition to walk. Owing to the character of the country and our enfeebled condition, we cannot hope to accomplish more than four or five miles a day on foot. As nearly as we can estimate, we are fifty or fifty-five miles from civilization (Wilson's ranch, twenty miles below the forks). We know nothing whatever of the river ahead of us, of the obstructions we will meet with, or even if we can get through at all by this route. The dreaded Black Canyon is yet before us. Worst of all is the fact that Colgate cannot possibly walk, and it is absolutely impossible to help or carry him around the bad places along the river. His condition grows worse hourly. His legs are in a frightful condition, and the odor that comes from them is almost unendurable. He is perceptibly weaker than he was yesterday, and his mind is so far gone that he has lately appreciated no efforts to make him comfortable.

On our return to camp at half-past two p.m., we drew to one side and discussed every plan that could be thought of—not a stone was left unturned. If we stay with him, we can do nothing but ease his last moments and bury him, because it is impossible for him ever to get well again. His sickness is, besides, of such a character that he might linger in a stupor or semi-conscious condition for several days, during which a large portion of our remaining provisions would be consumed. We cannot even take him back and leave him with Jerry Johnson while some of us go out on snowshoes for assistance. With no sign of game in the neighborhood and the river full of floating ice so that the fish will not rise, were we to leave half our provisions here and one man to care for Colgate, he would probably starve before succor could reach him, while such a drain on the meager supplies would render the chances considerably less of the others ever reaching civilization. We all feel that it is clearly a case of trying to save five lives or sacrificing them in order to perform the last sad rites for poor Colgate. To remain longer with Colgate is to jeopardize to the very doors of folly all our lives—not in the cause of humanity, for Colgate is beyond any appreciation of such kindness—but for sentiment solely. We have exhausted every resource and feel that we have gone to the extreme limit of duty toward Colgate in our endeavors to get him back to civilization. Our own families and friends have now a just claim upon us, and we have to save ourselves if possible. We therefore have decided to strike down the river, and, with good luck, some of us may get through unless we encounter a bad snowstorm. Everyone feels very much dispirited at having to leave Colgate. There is hardly a word spoken by anyone tonight.

Chapter XII

The Sacrifice

Sunday, November 12th — This morning we made up our packs, taking nothing but provisions, two flat stew pans that fitted inside one another, the smaller being filled with coffee, and two small frying pans. Abe took his camera, which is very light. I cut a roll of exposures out of mine and threw the box away. When we came to cross the river, we found it was not so easy as it looked. We had to reach a small point of rocks, fifty yards below us on the opposite side of the river. If we failed in this (and the current was against us, as it made in to our side of the river), we would be carried down into the big ledge, and that would be the end of us. Some were in favor of trusting to luck in trying to cross. If we got across, all right; if we didn't, all right too! Others proposed going down on our side of the river, but this was objected to on the ground that this side is likely not as open as the south-facing hillside and would have more snow. Besides, we would have to cross at the forks anyway, and while we had our rafts we had better cross here.

Abe suggested that we fell a very large white pine tree, which stood on the bank and seemed to lean toward the river, and by fastening a long rope to the end we could drift halfway across and then pull ashore with our sweeps while the rope held us from going down the stream. The tree was about forty-four inches in diameter. Keeley began the cutting. Others worked at various things, and I went hunting in the hope of getting some meat. I saw no fresh signs of game at all except one grouse. On my return I tried fishing with no better success. Our food for two days had been cornmeal and beans. It snowed a little today and was cloudy and cold. We start on our tramp tomorrow, taking nothing but provisions, guns, and the clothes on our backs.

Colgate is very bad tonight. He has great difficulty in breathing. It would not surprise me at all to see him collapse at any moment. I told him today that we could raft no farther and would have to walk, but it seemed to make no impression whatever upon him.

Monday, November 13th — Daylight found us up and through breakfast, and we were delighted to find it perfectly clear and cool. It took us until one o'clock to fell the big tree, as we had to fell another large tree against it and hitch ropes to its branches so that it would fall into the river. When it did fall, it fairly shook the earth, and to our disappointment, the top sank fifteen feet under the water. Still, the branches that were available reached nearly halfway across the river. Abe and Keeley tied one end of the long rope firmly to the limbs as far as they could reach, and the other end was fastened to the raft. We determined to test the strength of the rope and to land Abe on the opposite bank if possible, so that when we crossed with the big load we could throw him a rope, and he could help us land. Abe, Keeley, and I pushed off and got halfway across without the slightest trouble, but had to pull for dear life to get across the current. Landing Abe, we returned for the rest and made the trip safely, although we came close to an upset on account of the swift current, which nearly sucked one side of the raft down. After landing, we cut the raft loose to see where the current would take it. It was whirled downstream for two hundred yards and jammed into a mass of big rocks to the left of the middle of the river.

Poor Colgate was so far gone that he could not remember his family, nor did he make any remarks or request concerning them. We made him as comfortable as we could, left him what necessaries we thought he might require in the brief period he had yet to live and, shouldering our packs, we started sadly down the river. Although Colgate's head was turned toward us, he made no motion or outcry as he saw us disappear, one by one, around the bend.

We walked over some very rough country until we came to a small creek about two miles down, which we crossed on a log. Our path then led through a rather open flat, and we made camp on a small sandbar at about four o'clock, having walked two and one-half miles. A small, slanting shelter of pine boughs was made, under which we lay down to sleep.

Pine Bough Shelter

Tuesday, November 14th — We had a fairly comfortable camp last night and got several hours' sleep, which was doing well considering the cold and lack of all covering. After a breakfast of coffee and a small allowance of bread, we resumed our walk down the river at eight o'clock. We shifted and changed our packs a good deal today, as they begin to grow heavy and cut our shoulders. Besides our packs, Keeley carried an axe, and Abe, John and I had a gun apiece. The first part of the day our route was through a fine flat. We thought it was the flat below Bald Mountain, on which they say there is a warm spring. On a small side-hill we found a trail which led back into the mountains, and by the side of the trail some fairly fresh signs of Indian choppings and blazes. Some of us were anxious to stop for a day and get an elk, the fresh signs being numerous, but the majority favored going ahead, so we kept on.

After leaving the flat, the country began to grow rougher and the sidehills became steep, slippery, rocky, and brushy—all at once, as it were. On one of these side-hills we found an old line chopped out by a surveying party. The walking was very difficult, and we had to use both our hands and feet in climbing. We have kept an eye on the river and are satisfied that we were very sensible in abandoning the rafts. We have seen a good many places where we could not possibly have taken a raft through. About half-past one o'clock, we passed a fall of some six feet which had bad rocks above and below it. The river was beautiful. I had never seen such clear-looking water. We walked until three o'clock, having made, we think, five miles. Abe killed a grouse today, and I caught two fish weighing half a pound each. We enjoyed them hugely for supper, making broth from the grouse and frying the fish. Our camp is good, and we are fairly comfortable.

Wednesday, November 15th — We made a breakfast of tea and a little bread and started down the river at eight o'clock. The character of the country was somewhat the same as yesterday—small flats and very difficult sidehills. About noon we passed a fine large creek which runs through a deep gorge and flows into the river from the south. The lack of nourishing food, loss of sleep, and exposure are beginning to tell on us all; we are very weak and unsteady on our feet. Everything that will lighten our load has been thrown away. During the day we killed three grouse. Abe and John both had watches, but John's stopped after getting it wet in the river a week ago. For safety, Abe had been carrying his watch in his hip pocket. Today he slipped and fell down on a rock, smashing the watch. The crystal was pulverized so that it resembled salt. Our last and only timepiece was thus ruined.

We were caught at dark in a miserable flat some distance from the river, making it difficult to obtain water. It began to rain at dark and continued to rain, sleet, and snow all night. We had trouble securing firewood, and there was not a tree in the vicinity big enough to shelter anyone from the rain, so we got soaking wet and cold and had no sleep all night. The three grouse were stewed for supper and the bones given to the dogs, which had eaten hardly a mouthful since November 13th. They are about as weak as we are. Daisy, the black dog, seems to be in the poorest condition.

I feel that our chances are rather slim of getting out of the mountains. Everyone is tired and miserable.

Thursday, November 16th — We got up at daylight and partook of our usual slim breakfast of bread and coffee. The country was very rough today. The first part of our route was over broken, rocky shores. We found more perpendicular bluffs than usual, which we had to climb around. In our weak condition, we found it very hard work to climb up the steep hillsides. Our guns are a regular nuisance, for we need both hands in climbing. At half past ten we sighted the worst looking bluff we had yet seen and, upon coming to it, found our way blocked by a large and very rapid creek.

We stopped there and made a little coffee for lunch. Unable to find any tree on which to cross the creek, we were obliged to cut one down. Owing to the rain and sleet blowing down the river, the upper side of our tree was icy and slippery. Had anyone fallen off, he would have been swept down into the river and drowned. The water was so rapid that it was milky white from rushing over and between the rocks. Once across, we had a hazardous climb of an almost perpendicular sidehill for about one thousand feet. It was very slippery and icy, and we were all tired out on reaching the top. We were very lucky that no one fell.

Following the ridge for a quarter of a mile, we made a descent to the river again when, on turning a small point, we came upon the Black Canyon. There was no mistaking it this time! I do not think any view in the mountains ever impressed me as this one did. The view did not impress me so much with its grandeur as with an indefinable dread weirdness. It immediately associated itself in my mind with death. The river before us for several hundred yards was a broad, deep, still pool, which reflected perfectly the steep rocky bank opposite and the muggy sky above. The river gradually narrowed down as it approached the succession of mighty rock walls, which were so close together that they seemed to meet at the top. A hazy curtain seemed to hang before the tremendous gap, and behind this all seemed black. We could hear the sullen booming of the rapids in the distance, which had a peculiarly unpleasant sound, probably owing to their being enclosed in the huge rocky walls. I should judge that the highest point that we could see from there was at least three thousand feet above the river. I think we all realize that we have a difficult task ahead. We are very weak, and if Spencer is right in his belief that the canyon is eight or ten miles long, it will take at least two and a half or three days of hard climbing to get through it, if indeed it is passable at all.

We were so tired that it was decided that Abe, Spencer, and John should go down the river a short distance and select a suitable camp, while Keeley and I tried the fishing. Never had I seen a finer hole for trout, and in the clear water we could see fish of all sizes lying quietly here and there or swimming lazily about. We had no spoons and no large hooks. We had tied several small flies together and put a lead weight two feet in front of them to enable us to cast out, then we drew them slowly toward us. We hooked plenty of fish, but they were so large that they broke our hooks time after time. I am certain that one I had almost on shore when he broke my hook weighed at least five pounds—it was a Dolly Varden or bull trout. Keeley lost one that was considerably larger. After fishing for two hours and losing thirty or more fish and about twenty hooks, we gave up in despair and returned to camp with one half-pound trout which Keeley had landed. The others looked so disappointed when we returned to camp with only one small fish that we went out again and managed to catch two more, of nearly one pound apiece. These, added to the grouse Abe had shot, made us a first-rate supper. We stewed the fish, drinking the excellent broth, and divided the flesh evenly in our drinking cups. If we only had one good, strong trolling spoon, we could catch fifty pounds of fish easily.

Our camp is dismally cold and wet, but luckily we have plenty of wood near at hand. We made a big fire for the night. We saw that our best chance for food was fish, and after supper we hunted for something from which to make a spoon. Spencer produced a piece of copper wire, which he used to clean his pipe. Keeley made one spoon from the bowl of a teaspoon, while I made another by hammering out a silver half dollar. Money is some good in the mountains after all. They looked very good when finished and will undoubtedly attract the fish, but we still have to rely on the small hooks to hold them. Upon counting the hooks, I found that we have twenty-four left.

Friday, November 17th — We started at eight o'clock this morning, determined to do our best toward getting through the canyon. Our route led along a very steep, brushy hillside. We found an old game trail which slanted up the sidehill. We followed this until we were at an elevation of perhaps fifteen hundred feet above the river, when the trail was lost. I guess the game does not pass through the canyon but strikes back from the river into the hills. We had to be very careful of our footing, as the hillside was so steep that we would probably have landed in the river, or at any rate fallen over some of the numerous precipices, if we had slipped. The south side of the canyon is vertical at this point, and we believe that our side is so also at the river. It was almost vertical where we passed along today. We feel that we were very lucky to have crossed on the raft, for the walls opposite us are impassable. We found more snow today than we had yet seen, probably owing to the short time the sun shines in the canyon.

We continued walking with great care all day and made a difficult descent to the river in order to camp on a small point where we could get wood and water. Although we worked very hard, we have not accomplished more than two and one-half or three miles. Abe shot a blue grouse today. We made camp on the point and built a shelter to keep out the cold wind that sweeps down the canyon. It is necessary that we sleep all we possibly can to keep up our strength. The black dog looked so miserable tonight that I thought it the kindest act all around to kill her. This I did by shooting her in the head with Spencer's revolver. We then hung her up and skinned her, and when the flesh got cold, we cut off the best portions and made a strong broth—strong in every sense of the word. Into the broth we put a tablespoonful of flour. The soup was good, but the flesh was tough and strong. Although nearly starved, only one of the remaining dogs would touch the meat. By our camp is a very large, hollow cedar tree, the base spreading out over six feet. We made a fire in the hollow base. There was a strong draught, so we soon had a regular furnace going. The flames shot out of the top for some distance, and the heat finally became so great that we were obliged to leave our shelter and stretch out on the rocks. We found a portion of last summer's *Spokane Review* and a cleaning rod for a 45-calibre rifle on the spot where we made our shelter. Evidently someone was up the river this far last summer. We feel somewhat encouraged by these signs of man. Abe took several photographs today of the canyon walls and the "crowd." We tried fishing, but had no strikes.

Saturday, November 18th — We started out by climbing up the side of the canyon, taking every available chance to get forward. The walking was harder than any we had yet had. Many times we were stopped by high perpendicular faces of rock. We had to go up or down for considerable distances to get around some of these; others we had to cross and trust to luck not to fall. Keeley is particularly good at finding all available footholds and paths. He has been a splendid fellow all through, doing all he could and not grumbling at all.

Expecting to cut around some bad places, we climbed straight up for a long distance but found nothing better. We got into moose brush covered with snow, and our feet slipped from under us at every few steps. Nothing seems to do us so much harm in our weak condition as the jarring resulting from a fall.

After we got out of the moose brush, we ran into a thicket and then climbed a snowy sidehill through brush and downed timber. Looking back from the top of this ridge, we saw Bald Mountain about fifteen miles to the northeast. At three o'clock we struck what looked like a trail, but it led us to a point where there was a perpendicular descent of several hundred feet; it was evidently not a trail at all. The view from here was extended and grand, but we were not in a condition to admire scenery. We were utterly tired out and proposed camping. Spencer tried to get to the river, but came back and reported that he could not get down, so we decided to camp about fifty yards farther down in a bunch of rocks and near a little creek. It took me nearly one hour to work my way down to the creek and bring back a pail of water, but we found a much easier path later. We had difficulty in finding firewood for the night. A few boughs were cut to lie upon, but I fear no one will be able to sleep. We can easily see the rocky bluff just above last night's camp. We have made less than one and one-half miles down the river today. Everyone is growing weaker, and the flour is getting very low. Abe killed one grouse today, and tonight someone sang, "We'll be angels by and by," and no one seemed to disagree with the singer.

Sunday, November 19th — John decided to abandon his gun, so he left it hanging to a tree in camp. We felt that we must work hard today, which we did. We found occasional old game trails, and the walking improved. We lost much valuable time, however, by following one which took us up into the hills. We passed many bad places, and it is a wonder to me that no one slipped and fell, all being so weak. Two of us have no hobnails left in our boots, and three of us are very footsore. We feel encouraged by having seen that we are a good way below Bald Mountain, and we ought not to be more than fifteen miles from the forks of the river, where there is a trail leading down to Wilson's ranch.

Fresh deer signs were seen today. At four o'clock we reached the end of the canyon and camped near a small sandbar. We built two large parallel fires, but did not succeed in keeping warm. We have only enough flour left for one more meal. Not being able to sleep from weakness and cold, I sat thinking of what our friends were doing in the outside world, when my attention was attracted by the two little dogs, Montana and Idaho. Poor little Montana is very far gone, and so weak and thin that it is a surprise to me that she can keep up with us. All the hair is worn from her legs by the sharp rocks. Tonight she lay down as close as she could to the fire and extended her four legs, to keep them warm; still she shivered, I suppose from weakness. Idaho, her mate, is much stronger, and seemed to realize

Montana's condition, for she came and lay partly on top of her and partly on the outside of her, so as to protect the side exposed to the cold. I do not recall ever having heard of a similar case of animal sympathy.

Monday, November 20th — For breakfast we ate the last of the bread. We worked for all that was in us today and were favored with pretty good walking in comparison to what we have been having. We were able to keep near the river a good part of the time instead of having to continually climb around vertical walls. We staggered a good deal today from weakness, and Abe, who has stood it splendidly so far, is also beginning to break down, principally from lack of sleep, having averaged only about one hour a night for seven nights. We found a few frozen hawberries along our route, which we ate. Our violent cravings of hunger have left us somewhat, and our stomachs seem to have accustomed themselves to do with very little. Fully six miles were covered today, and camp was made during a cold rain in a damp flat. Abe went to look for deer for half an hour, but saw none, although fresh signs were plentiful in the snow. Keeley caught a fish weighing one pound, of which we made broth, and had that and coffee for supper. It was very difficult to get enough wood to last all night.

Tuesday, November 21st — We had a little piece of bacon, weighing about one-eighth of a pound, which we had used to grease the pan with in baking bread. The flour being exhausted, we made a broth of the bacon this morning. Abe went for deer, but got none, as it began to snow. Most of us were too weak to walk without breakfast and could barely stagger around. Keeley caught three fish which we ate, and we started down the river at eleven o'clock, walking very slowly and often stumbling and falling down. After going about a mile we found a nice fishing hole. Keeley caught four and I two, making six fine fish in all—a veritable feast. I had no control over my arms. When I whirled the spoon around to throw it into the river, it was just as likely to fly back of or above me. We soon made camp and stewed the fish. The dogs got quite a meal of fish bones and seemed to feel relieved.

Wednesday, November 22nd — It snowed about two inches during the night, and this morning it was dark and squally. We tried hard to catch fish, but did not get a strike. One small fish kept following Keeley's spoon to the shore but would not strike. Getting desperate, he shot at it with his revolver but missed. Seeing it was no use to fish, we made some tea and started slowly down the river.

The majority decided that we would walk no farther after today, but would try to build a crude raft if we could find light driftwood that required no cutting from which to build it. Our feet felt as heavy as lead, and falls were frequent. We noticed that the hills are getting very low now. Abe, who has been keeping account of our daily progress, estimated that we were about nine or ten miles from the forks this morning. The rapids are no longer dangerous, and most of us feel that, if we had a raft, we could make Wilson's ranch in a day or two at the most. If we could kill no grouse or trout, we could eat one of the dogs to keep up our strength.

The walking was rather hard, as we had to leave the riverbank to climb around vertical walls of rock several times. We had made perhaps one mile when we struck a particularly bad place. I got too high up to cross easily and thus dropped behind the others some distance, but found Abe waiting for me when I got down. I was tempted to throw away my gun, but disliked very much to part with it, as it is my favorite.

We continued slowly down along the sidehill and, seeing some hawberries on the riverbank, went down to eat them. I said, "Abe, it seems to me that our friends must know of our position, and that they would try to get up this river as far as they could toward us. They certainly know that this is the route we are most likely to take, and that we must be working down this way!" Abe said in reply, "I have thought it all over and believe they will send someone, but I allow them three or four days yet." On turning the next point, we saw two men hurrying toward us. Thinking they were of our party I said, "I wonder what's the matter? Perhaps they have seen a deer and want us to shoot it!" But he replied, "I am afraid someone has fallen into the river." As they approached nearer, we saw they were not of our party, and a moment later Abe recognized our old-time shooting chum, Sgt. Guy Norton of the Fourth Cavalry. With him was Lt. Charles P. Elliott. It expresses it mildly to say we were overjoyed to see them. Our tired limbs seemed filled with new life, and we followed them briskly to their first boat about two hundred yards below. Abe, who was very much interested in his estimate of distances, asked Mr. Elliott how far it was to the forks and learned with much satisfaction that the confluence of the south fork [the Selway River] with the Kooskooskee was about seven miles distant. When we arrived where Mr. Elliott's boat was lying, we found the rest of our party and two soldiers—Sgt. Smart and Pvt. Norlin, of Mr. Elliott's company—and three civilian boatmen, Messrs. Lamonthe, Burke, and Winn. They had a fire started and oatmeal and bacon cooking when we arrived. Mr. Elliott advised us to eat moderately at first until we gradually accustomed ourselves again to food. While enjoying our first meal, we learned all the details of the meeting of the two parties. Mr. Elliott's party was making its way up the river with two boatloads of provisions. So swift and rough was the water that a portage was necessary at nearly every rapid. They had gotten the smaller boat over the last rapid below, and while the balance of the party returned for the other boat, Mr. Elliott and Roary Burke sat down on a rock near the first boat and waited for them. While thus seated, their attention was attracted by the barking of Winn's dog, and when they looked around, Burke saw one of our little white terriers through an opening under the rocks. Not knowing what it was, Mr. Elliott asked for a gun, but soon discovered that what he saw was a small white dog. The terrier Idaho soon made her presence known by violent barking. At the same time Spencer, who had, however, seen the two men first, appeared above the rocks, followed closely by John and Keeley.

Mr. Elliot, seeing Spencer, accosted him with, "Hello! Who in God's name are you?"

Spencer replied, "My name is Spencer, the guide of the Carlin party. Who are you?"

After informing Spencer that a rescue party was at hand, Mr. Elliott asked, "How is everybody?" to which Spencer replied, "All well, but hungry as hell!"

The rest of Mr. Elliott's party having come up in the meantime, he left instructions to prepare a meal for the rescued party and came forward with Sgt. Norton, as already related.

Mr. Elliott immediately decided to send a courier with dispatches to Capt. Boutelle at Weippe and selected Mr. Winn. We were kindly given permission to send telegrams to our relatives and friends with the courier. We learned that new ranches had been built on the river above Wilson's, and that we were only five miles from the nearest cabin (King's). Mr. Winn will walk down the river to Hinds and Burke's ranch and thence ride by trail to Weippe.

Chapter XIII

The Rescue and Disbandment

After we had taken some refreshments on the river bank, all the provisions were ordered to be loaded in the boat, and the whole party, rescuers and rescued, returned to Mr. Elliott's last camp half a mile below.

Canvas stretched over poles afforded shelter, and while the civilians of Mr. Elliott's party went down the river to look for raft timber, the soldiers made camp comfortable and set about preparing the evening meal. No one who has not gone through a similar experience can imagine the feelings of rest, relief, and security that we felt sitting by the warm campfire with kind friends about us and plenty of food in sight.

Mr. Elliott inquired minutely about Colgate and was anxious to go after him and bring him out dead or alive. It was with great difficulty that we were able to persuade him that such a course was not only extremely dangerous but probably impossible.

From our knowledge of the river and the region we had just passed through, we knew the river was not navigable for boats above the mouth of the canyon, and ice floes were already forming, so that boating would probably have been impracticable above the point Mr. Elliott had reached when we met him. Assuming that to be the case, it would have been necessary to have the men who would volunteer to go carry twenty days' provisions on their backs and pass over the same route we had just traveled. Had no snow fallen during that time, they would in all probability have been able to pass through the canyon and reach the point where Colgate was last seen, but it would probably have been eighteen or twenty days after we had left him, and according to Dr. Webb's later statement, Colgate would then have been dead over fifteen days.

It would have been impossible in any case to bring out Colgate's body, as the canyon was absolutely impassable to the strongest men if burdened by such a load as Colgate's body would have been. Had snow fallen at any time while the men were in or above the canyon, they would have been hopelessly imprisoned and certainly lost, as there was no game of any kind in the canyon, and the snow, on the almost precipitous walls, would have rendered traveling so dangerous as to be practically impossible.

In view of the dangerous nature of such a trip and the fact that the burial of the body, if found, would be all the expedition could accomplish, Mr. Elliott wisely decided with us that the results did not warrant the jeopardizing of the lives of the valuable men who readily volunteered to go.

As it happened, four inches of snow fell at our camp the following day, and we believe that double that amount must have fallen in the canyon, which is much higher above sea level. It is therefore almost certain that an attempt to reach Colgate at that time would not only have resulted in failure, but might have ended disastrously.

In order that the boats could be made available to carry passengers, it was necessary to build a large raft to transport the provisions. The construction of the raft took nearly three days. This afforded us an admirable opportunity for recuperating and resting.

Mr. Elliott was exceptionally kind and considerate and repeatedly sacrificed his own comfort for us by giving us his blankets at night while he endeavored to sleep by the campfire. The first night in camp was, and no doubt always will be, a memorable night to us. For the first time in ten days we had a comfortable bed under shelter, and the sleep—the refreshing sleep which we so badly needed—was most delightful.

The weather was very disagreeable. It snowed and sleeted constantly, but we were all comfortable under the protecting canvas and happy in the thought that the anxiety of our friends would soon be changed into joy at the news that we were safe.

The day after we met Mr. Elliott, two trappers who were making a trip up the river reached the point where the men were building the raft. They had a canoe with a winter's supply of provisions, but became discouraged on account of the numerous falls and swift current of the river and decided to return to the forks and go up the south fork of the Kooskooskee.

The raft being finished on Saturday, November 25th, the provisions were moved down and loaded on it. Mr. Elliott, John, Spencer, and Lamonthe took the larger of the two boats, and Norton, Keeley, Will, and Abe the smaller one. The rest of the party manned the raft.

The start was made about eleven o'clock. The journey down the river in the boats was very interesting, and had the weather been fair and not quite so cold, it would have been greatly enjoyed.

The current, while not quite so swift as higher up the river, carried the boats along at a marvelous speed, and where the water was shallow, we could see the boulders shoot by beneath us, producing an effect similar to that of traveling on a railway train.

The river widened rapidly, the mountains on each side gradually became lower, and the fall of the river less. Shortly after we started, we passed the sluices and ruins of an old placer mining camp and soon afterward passed the first cabin, belonging to a man named King. Here Mr. Elliott stopped and returned some tools that had been previously borrowed. Continuing down the river a couple of miles, we reached the forks. Here the south fork [Selway] flows into the Kooskooskee. Several small falls were safely passed, but at about three o'clock, after having made a total run of perhaps twelve miles, we struck an ice floe which obstructed the river for several hundred yards. Mr. Elliott made an examination and found that the ice had formed an arch at the lower end of the floe which, if broken through, might allow the ice to pass off.

While his party were engaged in the work of disrupting the ice gorge, our party traveled down the river on foot, two and a half miles, to a ranch belonging to Roary Burke and F. M. Hinds. Mr. Hinds was at home and welcomed us very kindly. In half an hour we sat down to an excellent meal, to which we did ample justice. At sundown Mr. Elliott and party arrived with the raft and boats, having successfully broken through the ice floe. The ice passing out, after the breaking of the arch, was a spectacle well worth seeing—huge masses rising above the surface of the water and rolling over and over as the water became shallower below the pool where the gorge had formed.

Messrs. Hinds and Burke, in the role of hosts, acquitted themselves admirably, and the evening was pleasantly spent; cards, stories, and the incidents of the trip furnishing ample means of diversion.

It rained the following day, and as we were very comfortable in the capacious, well-built cabin, it was decided to remain there until the next day. In the morning, Messrs. Elliott, Burke, and Freeman and Sgt Norton went hunting, leaving at daylight, while the rest of us remained indoors and passed a quiet, restful day. At noon the hunters returned, having been unsuccessful in securing venison, but bringing in several grouse.

The next day, November 27th, at eight o'clock in the morning, we resumed our journey down the river. It rained all day, but we made excellent progress notwithstanding. After floating about eight miles down the river, we arrived at Kooskia [Sutler Creek], a post office where mails are received once a week. The postmaster had apples for sale, and we availed ourselves of the opportunity to purchase some and enjoyed them immensely.

The river constantly widened, and we passed into an open, rolling country almost destitute of timber. Only two stops were necessary to pass by dangerous rapids. At two o'clock we reached Kamiah, a Nez Perce Indian village, having made a run of about twenty miles.

Here we found an Indian trader's store, where we purchased some butter, cheese, and milk, which on trips of this character are always regarded as luxuries. We reembarked and continued down the river about a mile where we found a favorable place and made camp.

It continued to rain, but a comfortable camp with two large fires had a cheering effect, and everybody was happy. Although it was still raining in the morning, we broke camp at daybreak and continued down the river. Several dangerous rapids were passed, in one of which the raft came very near overturning. At another, the large boat, then occupied by Mr. Elliott, Will, John, and Lamonthe, was carried broadside against a large boulder and almost swamped. It was, however, pushed off in the nick of time, and it passed through the rapids with nearly a foot of water surging about in its bottom.

About one o'clock of that day we reached Greer's Ferry. Here Mr. Elliott met and reported to Capt. Boutelle. We also met Dr. Carter and Lt. Voorhees. The latter was an old acquaintance of Will's, and their meeting was to Will entirely unexpected. Mr. Voorhees was stationed at Fort Walla Walla, Washington, and had volunteered his services. In command of twenty picked men and with several wagonloads of supplies, he had arrived at Greer's Ferry several days before, only to learn that the lost party had been located by Mr. Elliott and was coming down the river.

An hour was spent at Greer's Ferry, when we re-embarked and continued down the river. At four o'clock, after having made a run of about eighteen miles, we reached the North Fork of the Clearwater. Here we made camp in the rain. Acting under orders from Capt. Boutelle, Mr. Elliott and party waited at that point until Capt. Boutelle joined him a couple of days later, while our party engaged passage from two ranchers in a covered wagon and traveled the following day to Snell's mill, eight miles distant.

Remaining there with Mr. Gainer overnight, we started the following morning on horseback for Kendrick. Six inches of snow had fallen during the night, and the morning was cold and clear. Mr. Elliott had kindly supplied us with warm army overcoats, so we had no difficulty in keeping comfortable.

It was fourteen miles to Kendrick. The last five miles were through a gulch or canyon leading from an elevated plateau to the valley of Bear Creek, which the railway follows. That portion of the highway is cut into steep hillsides, forming the sides of the gulch. The recent rain had swollen the stream and caused several landslides, making the road almost impassable at places. We, however, moved along without much difficulty, arriving in Kendrick at one o'clock—just in time to enjoy the Thanksgiving Day dinner at the St. Elmo Hotel.

Gen. Carlin had been in Kendrick for several days awaiting the arrival of the party, and the meeting of father and son was very affecting. A large crowd of interested spectators had gathered, which soon dispersed after our arrival.

The morning's ride in the crisp bracing air, after a week of rainy weather and insufficient exercise, proved very beneficial to all.

The following morning, December 1st, the whole party, including Gen. Carlin, left for Spokane, where we arrived about two o'clock. We were met at the depot by many friends, whose warm congratulations and hearty shaking of the hands conveyed the sincerity of their feelings.

The following day Dr. Webb, George Colgate's physician, was found. All the details of Colgate's illness and his condition at the time he was last seen were related to him, and upon request he made the following statement in writing:

> Mr. Colgate came to me from Post Falls last summer and I placed him in the Sacred Heart Hospital, where he remained about three weeks and then returned to Idaho. Early last fall he again came to me to be examined and said, if he was well enough, he would start on a hunting trip as cook. Mr. Colgate was troubled with an enlarged prostate and chronic inflammation of the bladder and had been for twenty years compelled to use catheters to relieve the bladder. I told him he could make the trip but to continue the use of the catheters, and from the history of the case and symptoms described by the Carlin party, I am satisfied Colgate's illness would have resulted fatally under any circumstances, and when he was left behind in the condition described, he would not have survived twenty-four hours.
>
> W. Q. Webb
> Spokane, Wash., December 4, 1893

Soon after our arrival we were met at the Hotel Spokane by Mrs. Colgate, Charles Colgate her eldest son, and several friends of the family from Post Falls. Will spent over three hours with them, telling the entire narrative of the trip and all the circumstances concerning Mr. Colgate. At the noon hour Gen. Carlin invited them to lunch, and after lunch a half-hour more was spent in relating additional details. After hearing the whole story, the accompanying friends were satisfied that all was done that could possibly have been done for Mr. Colgate.

It was suggested that a search party be sent out for the body, but we strenuously advised against such a course on account of the great danger and hardships incident to such an undertaking at that unfavorable season of the year. Will, however, volunteered his services and assistance in the spring, when a party could undertake such a trip with a reasonable hope of success.

Financially, as well as otherwise, the trip proved disastrous. Ben Keeley made considerable trouble by being dissatisfied and insisting on being paid a much larger sum than was originally agreed upon. Although Will offered to replace his personal property lost on the trip, besides paying the stipulated $250, he was dissatisfied, and finding he could not succeed in getting more, he accepted Will's offer, but went away angry and subsequently, when the party had disbanded, circulated the most cruel and malicious falsehoods concerning them. Although one of the rescued, he had the audacity to claim the reward offered by Gen. Carlin for the rescue of the party and threatened to bring a civil action against him for it.

All the camp equipage, except what was left with Jerry Johnson and what the party carried out with them, was irretrievably lost. The horses probably perished from starvation during the winter. A portion of the equipment that had been hired for the trip and which was returnable to the owners, had to be paid for. To all these pecuniary losses must be added the expense of the relief expeditions sent out by Gen. Carlin, which amounted to several thousand dollars.

On December 6th, after adjusting a few remaining business matters relative to the trip, the party disbanded.

With its disbandment, the story of the Carlin hunting party ends. As a hunting party proper, it met with very indifferent success. On account of the inclement weather, what game was taken was secured at the sacrifice of every personal comfort and much exposure. The disasters which befell the party are distinctly and directly traceable to a combination of two unfortunate circumstances: the premature fall of heavy snows in the mountains and the complete disability of George Colgate after the party had reached its destination. Had either of these misfortunes befallen the party singly, there probably would have been no more serious consequences than a little inconvenience or exposure for the members of the party, but both occurring simultaneously, the party found every resource by which the one misfortune could be averted, handicapped or rendered impracticable by the other.

The premature fall of the winter snows was a circumstance that could not, of course, have been anticipated, but the disability of Colgate was unquestionably due to his own folly in leaving behind the instruments on which his existence depended. By maintaining silence during the long journey into the woods, when a word would have halted the party and enabled them to inaugurate measures for his relief, he not only grievously wronged the rest of the party from an ethical standpoint, but also, as subsequent events proved, willfully threw away the only chance of saving his life and thereby sealed his own fate. When the party first realized the painful situation in which his conduct had placed them, they were, naturally, much chagrined, and although Colgate was a burden to them after the time they reached their permanent camp on the Kooskooskee, he was treated with the utmost kindness and, as he grew worse, nursed with the greatest care. When the return was attempted on October 10th, had it not been for Colgate's complete disability, the party would in all probability have continued their journey homeward on snowshoes over the Lolo Trail, arriving at Kendrick by October 20th. The anxiety of their friends and the expense of the relief expeditions would thus have been avoided, and the obligation of hazarding that month of privation and exposure occasioned by the journey down the Kooskooskee (the danger and hardships of which are as yet but half told) would not have devolved upon them.

It is doubtful if any other party of the same character and organized for a similar purpose was ever called upon to face such painful and desperate situations. Every emergency and crisis was, however, squarely and bravely met and carefully considered and discussed by the whole party in a most serious and rational manner, and the conclusions reached by them were prompted by a judgment based upon a knowledge of all the attending circumstances. That the rest of the party succeeded in effecting their escape down the Kooskooskee without serious or fatal accident falls little short of the miraculous.

Postscript

The Unwritten Code

From "Tragic Trek" by Edmund Christopherson, MONTANA, THE MAGAZINE OF WESTERN HISTORY, *Autumn, 1956.*

[Before the rescue]...the nation's newspapers were frantically registering despair for the unfortunate hunting party....There was immediate rejoicing when the messenger reached the tiny Idaho hamlet [Kendrick] with word of the rescue. "THE MOUNTAINS SURRENDER" headlined the first big news story of how the men had been snatched, more dead than alive, out of the jaws of death in the savage peaks of the Bitterroots.

The story was a thriller. Both the rescuers and the saved were heroes. Fresh from his 130-mile trip back from the spot where Elliott rescued the men, the courier told how, when found, the men presented a pitiable sight, being entirely out of provisions, barefooted, and with scant clothing. The little band of brave men were making their last and final effort to get out. Thirty-six hours more would have found them dead. The tragedy of Colgate's loss added the touch of pathos that made the whole affair especially satisfying to read and yarn about in the comfortable presence of a potbellied stove, or in warm, far-away living rooms.

News interest stayed at a high pitch. The story of the first interviews with the rescued party, a week after Elliott had rescued them, began with "THE ROMANCE IS ENDED. Poor Colgate is left to die. His remains to perish in the snow banks, and no attempt is made to rescue him."

Spencer's account of the incident ran:

> Colgate was unable to walk, and we could not use our snowshoes. Our predicament was now fully dawned upon us, and while we did not yet

lose courage, we readily realized the fact that only the greatest of luck could pull us out of those mountains alive. We built the rafts and encountered great difficulty for several days of rafting down the river. In five days of hard work we got 20 miles when we struck swift rapids and large boulders, and we could not possibly get through. Colgate was getting worse, his limbs were so badly swollen that he could not walk, and he had been delirious for some time. After getting across the river (to the side they were to hike downstream), we knew we could do nothing more for him, and it meant death to stay with him longer.

Fixing him as comfortable as possible and dividing our provisions equally with him (40 lbs. flour, 10 lbs. beans, 3 lbs. bacon), with plenty of tea, we knelt beside him and in fervent prayer we bade him goodbye. The snow fell pitilessly, and the weather was becoming extremely cold. We made a fire, placed wood within his reach, and came away, Colgate moaning, and amid his sobs making us promise to tell his family he died like a man. He begged of us that we should go and save ourselves, and so we left. This was on November 13. We resumed our journey, abandoning the rafts and going overland. This trip was as perilous as the one on water, for we constantly came in contact with boulders and jagged rocks, and the embankment was so abrupt and from 200 to 300 feet above the river that to miss our footing meant sure death. On the hardest day's travel, we killed five grouse and took sixteen small trout ...We were getting too weak to travel, the last three days we had nothing to eat but a few huckleberries and tea leaves. On the twentieth day I was ahead of the party about half a mile when I met Elliott and his party. It was a most joyous meeting, and you could plainly see tears trickle down our eyes.

Colgate was nearly dead when we left him. We knew it was no use to try to go up the river to find him. It would have been an impossibility to have done so, and while Elliott offered to make the venture, it would have proved suicidal. There was no way of getting back to the point from whence we came without going miles overland, and with snow falling at the rate of a foot a day, such an attempt was out of the question.

Himmelwright's version of the tragedy was:

The cook, Colgate, was with us in Coeur d'Alene five years ago and proved such a valuable and efficient man that Mr. Carlin wrote him and engaged him to go with us on this trip. When we arrived and found him feeble and sick, we endeavored to dissuade him from going. He insisted, and returned from a visit to his physician and assured us that he could go on the trip with perfect impunity, and that he was advised to go as it would be beneficial to his health.

When we started back, Colgate was unable to walk. Not wanting to take any chance of losing the man, after a consultation we decided to take him down the river on a raft. Had Colgate been well, and had we not been on account of his condition compelled to turn back from the Lolo Trail, we would have been out of the mountains by Nov. 1st. We hazarded an unknown river to give him every chance for his life. Building the rafts was slow work because we had to keep our fires up all night, and someone had to be up with Colgate. When we gave up rafting, Colgate crossed the river with us but was unable to proceed further, and we were compelled to leave him there upon the river bank. He was nearly dead. During the last 24 hours we were with him he didn't speak a dozen words. Our provisions were running out, and we had to keep on the move toward civilization.

As these accounts were published, there was an almost universal double take. The story of Colgate's abandonment left a bad taste. It seemed too much for some readers to swallow. Leaving a comrade, however hopeless his condition, was a violation of the unwritten frontier code that you stick with a companion in distress even though your own life may be forfeit. The abandonment took on an aspect of horror in the same dimension as grave robbing, the Donner Party's practical cannibalism, or the forsaking of grizzly-clawed Hugh Glass for dead by those Mountain Men who volunteered to stay and tend him. Public disgust with the party grew as the practical necessity for leaving 'poor old George' became seriously questioned by more and more people.

Men who knew the region said that the river bottoms were warm and well protected; that at no time does the snow reach such depths as to impede travel; that the river is easily navigable at all seasons. It seemed beyond reason that five able bodied men, in this predicament, should take more than five days to build two rafts, instead of the fourteen it took them. The desertion in print was soon called 'arrant cowardice.'

Keeley's explanation as to why it took so long to build rafts was that the two gentlemen amused themselves by hunting and fishing and didn't help. Colgate, he said, instead of being in a state of stupor and absolutely helpless when he and the rafts were abandoned, was on the contrary, considerably improved in health, though weak enough to greatly retard the party's progress. When they left Colgate, he continued, the five remaining men divided the provisions equally among themselves. They continued the journey with hardly a thought for their faltering comrade.

The New York hunters' story, and reputation, was hardly enhanced by another newspaper story to the effect that they received Colgate's widow with conduct marked by haste, indifference, and a degree of flippancy amounting to almost actual insolence. The sum of $25 was given to the son of the deceased as a final settlement of the account with his father. The men in the rescue party were dealt out a munificent $50. The Walla Walla, Wash., *Statesman* remarked editorially, 'The country has had a $50,000 fuss over $50 men.'

On Friday evening, Dec. 8, 1893 an entertainment was given at the G. A. R. hall in Colgate's home town, Post Falls, Idaho, for the purpose of providing aid for the widow and the seven Colgate youngsters, aged 2 to 17. Before the entertainment there was a meeting, 'remarkable for its earnest and orderly discussion of the circumstances, absence of heedless invective, and judicial spirit.' These resolutions were unanimously adopted:

> RESOLVED: That we hold Wm. E. Carlin and A. L. A. Himmelwright responsible for the management of the Carlin Party.
>
> That we express our thanks to Carlin and Himmelwright for the care and patience shown toward George Colgate—according to their published account—up to the hour when he was left behind.
>
> That we deplore the long delay on the river bank which the construction of the rafts does not explain—whereby time and food were wasted that should have been used for the sake of the sick companion in prompt and careful retreat.
>
> That we condemn the abandonment of George Colgate, while confessedly within a few hours of his death, and leaving him on his feet staggering in the snow without shelter, without fire, and without the presence of a loyal comrade to close his eyes and note the location of his body, as an act of hideous barbarity.
>
> That in the light of their own published statements and such other information as we can obtain, we denounce Carlin and Himmelwright as unfit to associate with sportsmen, wanting in the elements of manhood, and in their treatment of George Colgate's widow, wholly devoid of the considerate spirit and generosity of gentlemen.

The action of the relief party headed by Lieut. Elliott, in its failure or worse refusal to continue up the river after finding Carlin and his comrades, in quest of the abandoned Colgate is condemned and severely criticized by all. Backed as he was by a small army of men, provided with animals, provisions in ample quantity, and all necessary equipment for such work, there cannot seem to be any sufficient reason for his neglect to at least attempt the rescue of the deserted Colgate.

Conflicting accounts and responsibilities of the affair were hashed and rehashed all that winter and there was an unexpected volume of crossfire. In a later account, Keeley described how, on Carlin's orders, they told Colgate it was every man for himself. Although the poor fellow begged them not to desert him, Carlin was inexorable. Besides blankets and other gear being abandoned anyhow, they left Colgate with only a tin cup, some matches, and salt. He had his own fishing tackle. When later asked about the tin cup, Spencer said, 'We weren't particularly extravagant in furnishing Colgate with a drinking vessel, for we had tin cups to spare, and might as well leave the old man one as not.'

Further, the guide said in contradiction to his earlier and noble tear-jerking newspaper version, 'the reason that we did not leave Colgate what might seem to have been his rightful share of the little company's provender was that we did not think it would be of any assistance to him as he was too weak to have made any use of it, and we couldn't well afford to spare him any of our grub.'

Spencer added that he was not ashamed of his connection with the desertion, for he believed that others would have acted exactly as the Carlin Party did under similar circumstances. 'The direct and only cause of the unfortunate affair was the refusal of Carlin to comply with my wishes in regard to leaving the country when it commenced to rain and snow. [Leaving Colgate] could not be helped at the time, all recent published statements from alleged hunters and mountaineers to the contrary notwithstanding.' Spencer stated.

'They didn't even leave Colgate his dog to comfort him in his last hours,' Keeley bemoaned. He disclaimed personal fault on the grounds that he was a mercenary in the hire of Carlin and bound to do his bidding. Yet, he tried to claim a $2500 reward for rescuing the party!

Spencer, while confirming most of the details of Keeley's account, said that while journeying out, Keeley completely ignored Colgate, showing no interest in, or regard for, the sick man's well-being.

General Carlin called Keeley a blackmailer.

The newspapers defended Keeley. 'HAD IT BEEN YOUNG CARLIN, or one of his friends who had been deserted, instead of the party's cook, there is no doubt that Elliott would have reached him with his command, even though he would have to tunnel through forty feet of snow,' was one newspaper comment. A later version of the story had the party leaving Colgate with a revolver so, when the party had gone a distance, he could end it in the manner of disgraced frontier cavalry officers.

Colgate's doctor, a W. Q. Webb, of Spokane, gave some support to the contention that Colgate was near death when left. The physician described Colgate's ailment as an enlarged prostate and chronic inflammation of the bladder which for 20 years had compelled him to use catheters to relieve his bladder, and from the description of symptoms stated: 'he could not have survived more than 24 hours.' Present-day MDs give him more time, explaining that fluids Colgate was unable to void would first have been distributed in the tissues to create an affliction know as edema—the swelling of the legs, arms, and the whole body—which were Colgate's initial symptoms. Further surplus of fluid would be pumped into the lungs; hence his difficulty in breathing. And finally, uremic poisoning, with the characteristic failure to react to surroundings. Colgate was plainly in a bad way, but he might have lasted many days past the moment he was abandoned.

It was difficult throughout the winter of 1893-94 to escape talk of the Carlin Party. In one story that must have been opium-inspired, The New York *World* of Dec. 16, 1893, printed an account told by N. P. [Northern Pacific Railroad] brakeman John Mack, of how two trappers found Colgate wandering around the mountains in a heavy snowstorm, dazed and almost dead. After nursing him in a cabin they built, they were supposed to have taken him out to Lewiston, Idaho.

On December 27, one Sam Ellis, while dragging driftwood out of the Snake with the aid of a boat (near Penawa, 50 miles from Kendrick) glimpsed a bottle partially entangled in the wood he was rowing to shore. As he took his oar to shove it free he noticed that it was not empty. Further examination revealed a note purportedly from Colgate, dated Nov. 27, two weeks after the abandonment. Ellis was credited with sincerity, but the note, which referred to the 'lost Carlin hunting party' was generally conceded to be a fake.

In spite of the hazards of the winter, which were both adequately appraised and often exaggerated in the newspapers, seven distinct parties were organized to hunt for and bring out Colgate or his remains. Most of these washed out quickly once they got into the deep-snow country.

In February, 1894, Colgate's son Charles and three other men (including ex-Sheriff Bill Martin of Kootenai County, Idaho, and friend of Colgate's) set out on a heroic and heart-breaking journey up the river of his father's presumed death with 20-days' supplies on their backs. As if to prove the falsehood of Carlin and Elliott's rationalizations, they slogged upstream an estimated sixty-five miles past the point where Colgate was abandoned without finding a trace of the unfortunate victim. Their story was an epic of hardship. They stayed in more than forty days. Game was scarce. Food ran out. Their shoes and clothes wore out on the rocks and they used blanket strips wound around their feet for protection. While thus beset, one night, as the four huddled close to a fire they'd been building against a standing dead cedar, the tree collapsed, falling across Bill Martin, breaking his collar bone and mangling him painfully.

Here was a situation much like the one that the Carlin Party had faced earlier. The rescue expedition, too, had an invalid on their hands, unable to travel. They were now out of food, in hostile, bitter winter environment. But this group promptly fell to, built an improvised shelter and nursed Martin for six days until he was able to travel. Then, on an improvised litter, they carried him 35 miles to the first prospector's cabin. They continued to pack the invalid from shelter to shelter until they met the McLean party sent out to rescue them.

In March, two members of another four-man party, intent on rescuing or learning the fate of the elder Colgate, drowned in the Kooskooskee when their raft capsized in the rapid current.

Toward summer came another rash of Colgate-hunting expeditions. Carlin and Himmelwright and the Anaconda, Montana, *Standard* hired Spencer, Wright, and George Ogden to hike in from the Missoula, Montana, side on May 21st. They were to look for the remains, and, practically, to collect the gear and trophies that the party left with Jerry Johnson. They reported finding a tent and several blankets caught on driftwood near an eddy. Spencer found a roll of blankets weighted down by a boulder. He at once recognized this as the roll which had been done up for Colgate the previous fall. They had never been unrolled and the rope which had bound them to Colgate's back still held the roll together at one end. The other end of the rope was much frayed, as though worn through by rubbing against the ragged edge of a rock. One of Colgate's shirts was wrapped up inside the roll. About half-a-mile down river a sleeve, believed to belong to the corduroy coat which Colgate wore, was found hanging on the brush in the river. Yet further hunting for three more miles down river turned up no more evidence of Colgate or of his fate.

Unknowingly scooped by the rival *Standard*, the *Daily Missoulian* speedily hired Ben Keeley to return to the scene of infamy.

There was no warmth or camaraderie when Keeley and party, on the way in, met Spencer and party emerging. Spencer, who got out first, reported that Keeley had been lost. Wright, who had gotten bunged up and was resting at Johnson's cabin, told Keeley that he wouldn't find anything, intimating that he'd destroyed all traces of the various

Carlin campsites and that Keeley's mission would be fruit-less. He was right.

It remained for Lieutenant Elliott and a small expedi-tion of Army regulars, ostensibly on a mapping mission in the Clearwater, to turn up the ultimate evidence in the tragic case. Elliott and his command entered the Bitterroots via the northwest and made straight for the by-then-well-trampled-vicinity of Jerry Johnson's cabin. There the soldiers built a canvas boat and swiftly made the jour-ney along the campsites to the point where Colgate had been left to die. From this point Elliott's journey was more in the nature of a search. The river banks and treacherous country on either side of the wicked stream were carefully examined for traces of Colgate.

The search continued methodically. Downstream, eight miles from the spot where Colgate was abandoned, Elliott and his little band noted a small heap, the appearance of which was not in keeping with the surroundings. A close inspection revealed human remains. The grisly bundle con-sisted of a thigh bone, a portion of the thigh and a leg, bear-ing unmistakable evidence of having been mangled and gnawed by wild beasts. It appeared altogether likely that most of the body had been carried away by wild animals. Nearby were found a match box, fishing line, a piece of cloth, and other articles identified as the property of Carlin's unfortunate cook. Yet thorough search of the sur-rounding country failed to unearth any other portion of Colgate's remains.

Lt. Elliott then took the remains back to a spot on the north fork of the middle fork of the Clearwater [the Lochsa River] known as the lower hot springs (where the Carlin Party first built their rafts) now called by some Colgate Warm Springs, and there interred them with such solemnity as was possible under the circumstances.

A little mound of rocks and earth, neatly rounded with a headboard rudely constructed of a large split cedar, bear-ing the simple jackknife-carved inscription GEORGE COL-GATE, told the story of a man cruelly deserted by five human beings.

Appendix A

The Relief Expeditions

Early in November, 1893, after deep snows had been reported in the mountains, Mr. John L. Randle of Spokane, Washington, received the following characteristic and significant letter from William H. Wright of Missoula, Montana:

> If Spencer has not got out of the mountains before now, he will not get out before spring— not that way [via Kendrick], as the snow is from four to six feet deep in the mountains and it is impossible to get out any horses unless it is this way [via Missoula]. Even then one could not do so unless they went in from this way and took a packtrain of oats. It has snowed for over a month on the range. I came out with a party in about two feet of snow. Two men going out about a week ago started with six horses and got out with two, and would not have got out then only for some Indians who helped them. Do you know of anyone who knows where they [the Carlin party] were going and how much grub they took? How many horses did they take? General Carlin had better send out a relief party to hunt them up. If you see him, tell him I really think so, for if they have not got out they will not, unless they come on snowshoes.

As Mr. Wright was a well-known professional guide and a partner of Martin P. Spencer, the guide of the Carlin party, the letter was deemed highly important and promptly handed to Capt. Louis Merriam, U.S. Army, also of Spokane. Capt. Merriam immediately telegraphed Mr.

Wright for further particulars and received a reply to the effect that nothing had been heard of the Carlin party and that six feet of snow was reported in the mountains. Capt. Merriam then telegraphed Gen. Carlin, apprising him of the situation. This took place on November 7th. The same evening Gen. Carlin replied as follows:

> Thanks for information. If possible, go to Missoula and ask Colonel Burt, commandant at Fort Missoula, for a party of men, pack animals, subsistence, and guide, and go to relief of Will and party. I will pay all expenses.

On account of a washout on the Northern Pacific Railroad, Capt. Merriam was delayed at Hope, Idaho, until Lt. Martin, aide-de-camp of Gen. Carlin, had reached the same point from Vancouver en route to Missoula with identical instructions. Capt. Merriam thereupon returned to Spokane to direct the movements of the other parties, while Lt. Martin pushed his way eastward toward Missoula, where he arrived on the morning of November 10th. After consultation with Maj. McKibbin (Col. Burt being at that time absent), it was decided to send a strong relief party into the mountains.

In the meantime, Lt. Charles P. Elliott, of Troop E, Fourth United States Cavalry, hearing of Gen. Carlin's apprehension for the safety of his son and party, kindly volunteered his services to go to their rescue. Accompanied by Sgt. Smart and Pvts. Markland, Norlin, and Ruhl, they arrived in Spokane from Vancouver Barracks on November 9th. His instructions were to go via Fort Sherman, increase his command to ten men, and complete his supplies for a winter's campaign, and then proceed to Saltese, Montana, via Old Mission, and cooperate with the relief party from Missoula. On reaching Old Mission, he found telegraphic orders awaiting him recalling him to Fort Sherman and instructing him to proceed to Kendrick, Idaho, join Lt. Overton's party at that point and endeavor to penetrate the Clearwater wilderness from the west.

Lt. Overton, of the Fourth Cavalry, with four troopers and a packtrain, had already arrived at Kendrick via Colfax and moved on toward Weippe. Lt. Elliott, on his arrival at Kendrick, proceeded at once to Weippe, where he found Lt. Overton busily engaged in preparing for a journey over the Lolo Trail. Lt. Elliott, on the other hand, resolved to attempt an ascent of the Kooskooskee and on the morning of November 14th started for Kamiah. The same day Capt. F. A. Boutelle arrived at Weippe and assumed command of all the military parties entering the mountains from the west.

While these movements were taking place on the western border of the Clearwater wilderness, a detachment of fifty-three men, under the command of Captain Andrews, of Company F, Twenty-fifth Infantry, was penetrating the same region from the east. This force left Fort Missoula on the afternoon of the 10th of November, taking three escort wagons and rations for fifteen days. They were followed by Lt. Devol, Lt. Martin, William H. Wright (guide), two packers, one supply wagon, and two pack mules. Great difficulty was experienced in passing the numerous fords of Lolo Creek, and the supply wagon was finally abandoned and the stores transferred to the pack mules. After reaching the Lolo Warm Springs on November 12th, a reconnaissance was made to the divide, and on the following day another to the Kooskooskee [Lochsa River].

Three stations, numbered 1, 2, and 3, were then established on the trail west of the Warm Springs, the last being on the Kooskooskee. Five men and two pack mules were to occupy each station and make daily trips over the intermediate portions of the trail, keeping it open and transferring provisions, orders, etc. These stations were established on November 15th, and the following day Mr. Wright, accompanied by Lt. Caldwell and two men with four pack mules, started down the old Indian trail along the river toward the camp of the Carlin party.

The ice in the bed of the river and the difficult fords, in which the mules were swept off their feet by the swift current, made their progress so slow that at the end of six hours they found they had only accomplished two miles. Owing to the necessity of cutting loose the packs in order to save the mules from drowning when they fell in the river, nearly all their provisions and forage had been lost.

Mr. Wright lost his gun and came very near being drowned by his horse slipping in the river and falling upon him. Under these circumstances the route down the river was pronounced impracticable, and the party returned to Station No. 3, on the river, whence they had started in the morning. The next morning, November 17th, the same party attempted to reach the Carlin party's camp by way of the Lolo Trail over the mountains. No serious difficulty was experienced for the first five or six miles, except that the snow became deeper and deeper as they proceeded. At that distance, however, they found the snow on the north hillsides so soft that the horses could not travel in it, while the south hillsides were so steep as to be absolutely impracticable for horses. They were consequently compelled to return again to Station No. 3 and decided to send to Capt. Andrews for enough men and mules to establish two more camps beyond the Kooskooskee and then attempt to reach the Carlin camp on snowshoes.

Capt. Andrews was at Station No. 1, and on the arrival of Lt. Martin and Mr. Wright, he informed them that high water had rendered the wagon road impracticable and that their supplies were cut off. Only two days' provisions remained, and a snowstorm was approaching. Capt. Andrews therefore sent out couriers to recall the men at the other stations, and on the night of November 18th the whole force had collected at the Warm Springs. The next morning a snowstorm was raging, and it was decided to return at once to Fort Missoula. The high water still rendered the wagon road impracticable, and all the wagons and many of the supplies had to be abandoned. Everything that could be taken was carried on the pack animals over the high-water trail, which was extremely dangerous at that season of the year. Five of the mules at different times lost their footing and rolled headlong down the steep sides of the mountains along which the trail passed. One of these rolled a distance of at least five hundred feet, striking the snow at intervals of about every fifty feet. He was found shortly afterward browsing on the brush in the most unconcerned manner near where he had fallen, but very little of his pack was recovered. Two of the other mules were killed, however. The expedition returned to Fort Missoula on November 24th, and two days afterward the telegraph announced the rescue of the party.

While Capt. Andrews' command was struggling in the deep snow on the east, Lt. Overton was pushing his way laboriously into the mountains on the west. Lt. Elliott had, in the meantime, proceeded to Pete King Bar on the Kooskooskee, where several days were spent in building two boats. When these were completed, provisions for an all-winter campaign were loaded into them and the journey up the river begun. At noon of the second day, November 22nd, they had reached a point about five miles above King's cabin and about seven miles above the confluence of the Kooskooskee and its south fork [Selway River], where they met the half-famished survivors of the Carlin party, as already described.

Upon the receipt of the dispatches sent by Lt. Elliott, to the effect that the Carlin party had been found, all the search and relief expeditions were immediately recalled.

Appendix B

The Phenomenal Precipitation of
Rain and Snow, Autumn 1893

The vast region between the Coeur d'Alene and Bitterroot Mountains on the east and the Cascade Range on the west was subjected to a most phenomenal rainfall in the autumn and early winter of the year 1893. It was naturally more conspicuous and more carefully noted in the agricultural sections of the region where, in many instances, the early, heavy, and incessant rains seriously interfered with the harvesting and housing of the crops. The Palouse country—famous the world over for its productiveness—lying directly west of the Bitterroot Mountains and adjacent to them, was, for the first time in the recollection of the oldest inhabitants, deluged with rain. The ground soon became soft and miry, so that it was impossible to haul the grain out of the fields after it had been harvested. Consequently over two hundred thousand bushels of grain soured and were lost in the fields of this section alone.

The deepest snow ever known fell in the mountains. In the Cascade authenticated depths of thirty to thirty-five feet were reported, and in the Bitterroot and Coeur d'Alene Mountains corresponding depths of twenty to twenty-five feet. It is well known by the ranchers and mountaineers living on the outskirts of the Clearwater wilderness, that the winter snows usually begin to fall after the 15th of October, and that it is unsafe to remain in the mountains later than that time. There are, however, a number of instances in which prospectors and hunters have succeeded in getting out of the mountains as late as the last of October. Among these may be mentioned the case of Dr. C. S. Penfield, of Spokane, Washington, who hunted in the Warm Springs locality on the Kooskooskee the previous year, 1892, and in 1891. On the latter occasion he returned over the Lolo Trail, reaching Kendrick after encountering only two feet of snow, as late as October 23rd.

In 1893, however, the snows in the Bitterroot Mountains began to fall as early as September 18th. No apprehension was felt so early in the fall, and it was not until about the 5th of October that the steady rain and snows caused alarm to persons belated in the mountains.

In September, Messrs. Larson and Houghton assisted Jerry Johnson and Ben Keeley to pack in the winter's supply of provisions to their cabin near the Warm Springs on the Kooskooskee. On September 27th, the day after the Carlin party had arrived and made their camp, Messrs. Larson and Houghton started to return to Missoula with a number of the pack animals. It will be remembered that on this day the prolonged rainstorm began, as noted by the Carlin party. After leaving the river bottom, Messrs. Larson and Houghton found themselves in a raging snowstorm, which, continuing with unabating fury, rapidly increased the depth of the snow on the trail. At one time during their journey, notwithstanding that their horses carried little or no burden, they had almost abandoned them, their progress being so slow and difficult. After four days of continuous floundering in the snow, during which time the snow had fallen to a depth of three feet, they reached the Lolo Warm Springs in Montana, in a state of complete exhaustion.

By the 10th of October the snow was five feet deep on the Lolo Trail. When the relief expeditions endeavored to pass the mountains early in November, the snows had piled up to a depth of eight to ten feet.

In light of these facts, it would appear that the Lolo Trail became impassable for horses on account of the deep snow about the time the Carlin party had reached their destination on the Kooskooskee.

Appendix C

The Search for Colgate's Remains

On December 27, 1893, a bottle containing a letter purporting to have been written by George Colgate and bearing the date November 27th, was taken from the Snake River near Penewawa, sixty miles below Lewiston, Idaho. Notwithstanding that it was impossible to properly authenticate the letter, and that it contained the phrase, "Lost Carlin Party" (which was of newspaper origin), many persons living in the neighborhood of Post Falls and Kendrick believed that it was written by Colgate.

Contrary to the advice of everyone who was acquainted with the dangerous character of such an undertaking in midwinter, seven distinct parties were organized to search for and bring out Colgate or his remains. With inadequate outfits and unacquainted with the character of the country, the most successful of these spent two months in the mountains, enduring the most painful hardship and exposure, only to find that the deep snow rendered the success of their undertaking hopeless.

In March, 1894, one of these parties met with a fatal accident. Four men had gone up the river to trap and look for Colgate. They ascended the river in a canoe to a point near the Black Canyon, but finding the snow still very deep and their progress slow and laborious, they decided to return. An attempt was made to run the rapids in the canoe, but they had gone only a short distance when the canoe ran into a log and was smashed. Some of their supplies were lost, but they removed the remainder to the nearest bank and improvised a rude raft. Starting out on this, with two men at each end, they had proceeded only about eighty rods when the raft struck a rock in the river, and the two men at the forward end of the raft were thrown into the rapid current. Although they were strong, active men and good swimmers, they failed to reach the shore and were drowned. The other two men clung to the raft and the rocks, and by cutting one log of the raft loose at a time and tying them together with their coats and shirts, managed after two hours of peril to reach the shore. The names of the two men lost are Loyal C. Hallam and Harry Gamble. The former was about twenty-seven years of age and had a mother and sister living at Humbolt, Nebraska; the latter was of about the same age and came from Baker City, Oregon. The bodies of both men were subsequently found—one near Kooskia P. O. and the other near Lapwai [Spalding], where they were buried. Both men were unmarried.

In the spring of 1894, Messrs. Carlin and Himmelwright engaged Martin P. Spencer to undertake a journey to the cabin of Jerry Johnson at the earliest date at which the journey could be made with safety. The object of the expedition was to search for the remains of George Colgate and recover the camp equipage, etc., which had been left with Johnson. Mr. Spencer secured for companions his partner, William H. Wright, and George R. Ogden of Missoula, Montana, and started into the mountains on May 21st. After experiencing considerable difficulty with snow (which at places was twenty feet deep, but packed so that the horses were enabled to walk over it) and high water, they reached Jerry Johnson's cabin on June 7th. Old Jerry was delighted to see them, having endured seven long months of solitude. His provisions were almost exhausted. The snow had been ten feet deep on the little flat where his cabin stood and where the Carlin party had encamped the preceding fall. For two and a half months he had been imprisoned in his cabin by the soft snow, coming out only to secure necessary firewood, which was near at hand. His little terrier dog, Tootsey, had been his sole companion all winter. After the snow had melted sufficiently, he secured some game and succeeded in trapping a few fur-bearing animals.

All the horses which the Carlin Party had left there and three belonging to Johnson had died during the winter, but the trophies and camp equipage which had been left in the cabin in Johnson's care were found in good condition.

On June 10th, the party started down the river in search of Colgate's remains, taking two pack animals. Two days of difficult work over an old trail and the loss of one of the pack animals brought them to a point eighteen miles below Johnson's cabin. Here the riverbank became impracticable for horses. Starting out the next morning on foot, six hours of hard climbing were required in order to pass over the remaining five miles to the last camp of the Carlin Party. On their arrival at that point they saw the tent and several blankets caught in some driftwood in an eddy. Near the same place were more blankets, on the sand about five feet from the edge of the water. A short distance farther downstream the party found a roll of blankets Spencer identified as having belonged to Colgate. The sleeve from a coat was discovered about a half mile below the blanket roll. Although the search was prosecuted with the utmost care and diligence for three miles farther down the river, nothing more of the unfortunate Colgate was revealed. Returning to Jerry Johnson's cabin, the party rested two days and then returned to Missoula, where they arrived on June 21st.

The facts developed by this expedition seem to indicate:

1. That the unfortunate man was unable to move any appreciable distance from the spot where he was last seen.

2. That since his blankets had not been unrolled, he probably never regained the full power of his faculties, but remained in a semi-conscious condition until his death.

3. That all the facts ascertained by this expedition, as well as his condition and all the circumstances surrounding him when last seen, indicate almost to a certainty that George Colgate died within twenty-four hours after the departure of the other members of the party; and from the nature of his ailment, death must have come to him without conscious pain.

4. That the high water in the spring carried the body downstream.

United States Army expeditions were sent out by the Dept. of the Columbia to explore the St. Joseph and Clearwater River basins. To one of these expeditions, in command of Lt. James A. Leyden, was assigned the territory north of the Lolo Trail, and to the other, in command of Lt. Charles P. Elliott, the region south of the Lolo Trail. During the month of August, while on the Kooskooskee River, Lt. Elliott found and buried the remains of George Colgate. The unfortunate man's remains were found about four miles farther down the river than the Spencer-Wright search party had gone and about eight miles below the place where they had found his blankets the preceding June.

Also From
Mountain Meadow Press

CLEARWATER COUNTRY, THE TRAVELER'S HIS-
TORICAL AND RECREATIONAL GUIDE; LEWIS-
TON, IDAHO—MISSOULA, MONTANA, by Borg
Hendrickson and Linwood Laughy. (Mountain
Meadow Press, 1990)

IN PURSUIT OF THE NEZ PERCES; THE NEZ
PERCE WAR OF 1877; as told by General O. O.
Howard, Duncan McDonald, Chief Joseph. Compiled
by Linwood Laughy. (Mountain Meadow Press, 1993)